Adam Sandler
Celebrity with Heart

Michael A. Schuman

Enslow Publishers, Inc.
40 Industrial Road
Box 398
Berkeley Heights, NJ 07922
USA

http://www.enslow.com

To Frank Barndollar, one funny man
and the sage of the Monadnock Region.

Library of Congress Cataloging-in-Publication Data

Schuman, Michael.
  Adam Sandler : celebrity with heart / Michael A. Schuman.
    p. cm. — (Celebrities with heart)
  Summary: "A biography of American comedian and actor Adam Sandler"—Provided by
publisher.
  Includes bibliographical references and index.
  ISBN 978-0-7660-3402-0
  1. Sandler, Adam—Juvenile literature. 2. Actors—United States—Biography—Juvenile
literature. 3. Comedians—United States—Biography—Juvenile literature. I. Title.
  PN2287.S275S38 2010
  791.4302'8092—dc22
  [B]
                              2009023806

ISBN: 978-1-59845-202-0 (paperback ed.)

052010 Lake Book Manufacturing, Inc., Melrose Park, IL

Printed in the United States of America

10 9 8 7 6 5 4 3 2 1

To Our Readers: We have done our best to make sure all Internet addresses in this book
were active and appropriate when we went to press. However, the author and publisher
have no control over and assume no liability for the material available on those Internet sites
or on other Web sites they may link to. Any comments or suggestions can be sent by e-mail
to comments@enslow.com or to the address on the back cover.

Every effort has been made to locate all copyright holders of material used in this book.
If any errors or omissions have occurred, corrections will be made in future editions of this book.

♻ Enslow Publishers, Inc., is committed to printing our books on recycled paper. The
paper in every book contains 10% to 30% post-consumer waste (PCW). The cover board
on the outside of each book contains 100% PCW. Our goal is to do our part to help young
people and the environment too!

Illustration Credits: Associated Press/ Wide World Photos, pp. 47, 49, 92; Everett Collection, Inc. pp. 4, 7, 39, 56, 62, 69, 72, 74, 79, 82, 84, 96, 104; From the collection of Bill
Dow, pp. 11, 14, 17, 19, 21, 23, 25, 26; Nathan Makan, p. 31.

Cover Illustration: Associated Press/ Wide World Photos

Contents

Staring Into the Hotel Room Mirror

Adam Sandler has a gift—the ability to make people laugh. However, in 1989, he was unable to share that gift with many people. He was telling jokes in small nightclubs and he had even gotten small parts in movies. But he had bigger plans. He wanted to entertain a lot more people. He wanted bigger parts in movies. He knew there was one stage where he could reach tens of millions of people at one time. That would be in the cast of *Saturday Night Live*.

Saturday Night Live, or *SNL*, is a comedy and variety program that airs on NBC at 11:30 P.M. eastern time on Saturday. Each individual program's host is a different celebrity. It could be someone in the world of show business, sports, politics, or business. But it is the same crew of actors who support the host in skits on every show.

As its name indicates, the show always airs live. It is one of very few television programs, other than sporting events and news, to broadcast live. *SNL* premiered on October 11, 1975. It has since become an American favorite. Sandler recalled:

> I was in, I think, sixth grade when *Saturday Night Live* was the biggest thing. I'm sure the other guys who are my age probably said this too, but my big thing was trying to stay up to watch it.
>
> The show was a major part of the life of every one of the kids I grew up with. It was not only topical, because it dealt with current events; it was just like instilled in our heads. "These are the funniest guys of our generation, so whatever they say is funny is funny."[1]

Sandler was desperate to be one of those funny guys.

When they are hired, most of the *SNL* cast members are not famous. However, many have used their stints on *SNL* as a springboard to huge careers in the movies or on television. These big names include Will Ferrell, Mike Myers, David Spade, Eddie Murphy, Jane Curtin, Julia

The second season cast of *Saturday Night Live*: John Belushi, Dan Akroyd, Bill Murray, Laraine Newman (back row, left to right), Gilda Radner, Jane Curtin, and Garrett Morris (seated front, left to right). The only cast change from the first season was the addition of Murray, who replaced Chevy Chase.

Louis-Dreyfus, Tina Fey, Chris Rock, Tracy Morgan, Dennis Miller, and Amy Poehler.

Sandler had hoped that if he could make the cast of *SNL*, he might someday become as famous as Eddie Murphy or Bill Murray.

Meanwhile, he kept doing his gigs in comedy clubs in California and New York. Finally, Sandler got the break he was looking for.

There are different versions of Sandler's first break. One is that Sandler was performing one night in a Los Angeles comedy club called The Improv. (Improv is short for "improvisation," or making up comedy material on the spot rather than using pre-written jokes.) Sandler liked to improvise onstage as well as tell jokes he wrote in advance.

Some say that in the audience that night was *SNL* cast member Dennis Miller. Miller found Sandler's performance hilarious. He then told *SNL* creator and producer Lorne Michaels about this young comedian who tells weird jokes and acts crazy onstage. Michaels flew Sandler not to New York but to Chicago where he was auditioning comedians for *SNL*. Chicago has always been fertile ground for discovering young comics.

Another story goes this way. Like most entertainers, Sandler has a manager. The purpose of a manager is to help a performer advance his or her career. This version of Sandler's big break has nothing to do with Miller or any other comedian discovering him. Sandler's manager contacted *SNL*'s producers many times until they decided to give him an audition. Sandler then flew to Chicago to try out for the show.

As most people would be, Sandler was nervous before the interview.[2] Although he enjoyed improvising, Sandler wrote an outline for his audition. He stared into his hotel room mirror the night before and told himself he better not choke.

That was not a problem. Sandler blew away the *SNL* staff. He was hired to work for *Saturday Night Live*.

However, he was not hired as an actor. He was selected to be a writer. He would write skits for the cast. But this was a first step to making his dream come true.

"He Was Full of Mischief, He Was an Underachiever, He Was Brilliant"

Adam Richard Sandler was born on September 9, 1966, in Brooklyn, New York. His father was an electrical engineer named Stan. His mother, Judy, was a stay-at-home mother. Adam has an older brother named Scott and two older sisters, Elizabeth and Valerie.

The Sandler family lived in an apartment in a neighborhood called Brooklyn Heights. One of his earliest memories is his mother's home-cooked meals, especially her meaty lasagna. He used to make his mother laugh by going around the family apartment and imitating his father's unusual sneeze. Sandler said it made a sound like "ayeestra."

When Adam was five his father took another job, which meant the family had to move. Adam's new home was Manchester, New Hampshire, about two hundred miles north of Brooklyn. Manchester is a very different city. Brooklyn is a sea of humanity with more than two million residents.[1] By contrast, roughly one hundred thousand people live in Manchester—the same number of people that live within a single neighborhood in Brooklyn.[2]

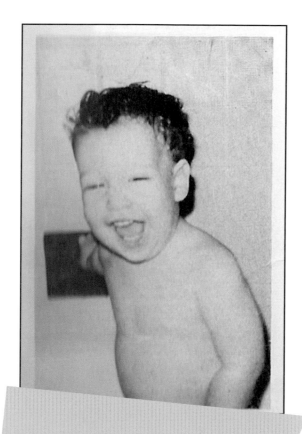

Adam Sandler as a baby in 1967.

Manchester is hardly a small town. It is the biggest city in New Hampshire. But the move to Manchester was an adjustment for Sandler. Brooklyn is a hugely diverse city with people from all cultures. The Sandlers are Jewish. About half a million Jews live in Brooklyn.[3] The largest ethnic groups in Manchester are French-Canadian and Irish. There is a sizable Jewish minority, but it is a small part of the total population.

All five-year-old Adam knew was that he was moving to a city far from his world of friends and comfort. Adam's father helped him feel better by telling him that there were really good toy stores in Manchester. He added that they sold lots of G. I. Joe action figures, his favorite toy.

Late in the summer of 1972, the Sandlers made the big move. In Manchester, the Sandlers would live not in an apartment but in their own house. Adam shared a bedroom with his brother while his two sisters shared their own bedroom.

Adam entered the first grade in September. His school, Webster Elementary, was tucked in the woods. It was also within walking distance of his new home.

When it was time for recess on his first day at school, Adam went outdoors with the other children. But while the other children stopped on the playground to play games, Adam kept walking. He did not stop until he reached his parents' house. He started crying and said he did not want to go back to school. His mother made him lunch, then took Adam back to his classroom.

That did not make Adam any less scared of school. One classmate, Bill Dow, remembered what Adam's morning routines were like for a few weeks. Dow said, "His mother would walk him from their car to his desk. He'd get really upset. As soon as she left he would escape. He'd hide in the woods adjacent to the school."[4]

Dow said that because he had a friendly manner, he was often chosen to find Adam and bring him back to class. Dow said, "I just talked to him. I'd say I don't know what you're scared of. It's all fun and games here. There's nothing to be scared of. He wouldn't answer to teachers, but he would answer to me."[5]

After awhile, Adam began making friends with his classmates, including Bill. Adam gradually became more comfortable and stopped trying to run away.

Dow said about young Adam, "He was always a storyteller. He'd tell a lot of tall tales. We would take what Adam said with a grain of salt. He'd say, 'My father went to Arizona.' His dad really did go to Arizona, but instead of just saying, 'My dad went to Arizona,' he'd say, 'My dad went to Arizona and was fighting rattlesnakes.' In first grade we'd believe it and say, 'Wow, your dad was fighting rattlesnakes!' Adam's father would say, 'Oh, Adam's telling his tall tales again.'"[6]

Comedian Rodney Dangerfield (above), famous for his constant complaining that he received "no respect at all," was a favorite performer of the Sandler family when Adam was growing up.

When Adam was about seven, the Sandlers took a family vacation to a resort in the Catskill Mountains in New York state. The Catskill resorts are popular destinations for many Jewish families. Many hotels and resorts elsewhere practiced for decades a form of discrimination called "restriction." They restricted their guests to Christians, refusing to accept Jews. While much restriction of that sort had ended by the 1970s, the Catskills remained popular with Jewish vacationers.

Guests at the resorts often went swimming or played tennis during the day. At night they were entertained by famous comedians. Adam sat and watched his father and older brother laugh hysterically at the comedians. While Adam was too young to understand the comedians' jokes, he always remembered how the audience laughed heartily during their acts.

At home his father liked to listen to comedians on phonograph records, long before the days of compact discs. Two of his favorites were Jewish comedians Mel Brooks and Rodney Dangerfield. Dangerfield's specialty was the one-liner, a joke that was literally told in one line. His catchphrase was "I don't get no respect."[7] One of his famous one-liners concerned his childhood: "I played hide and seek; they wouldn't even look for me."[8]

Sandler later said, "My favorite comic, when I was getting into it, was Rodney [Dangerfield] . . . I'd walk around my house doing Rodney jokes for my dad, and he would laugh."[9]

Dangerfield rarely if ever mentioned being Jewish in his comedy routines. On the other hand, Brooks told a lot of jokes about being Jewish. However, one of Mel Brooks's most famous routines is called the 2,000 Year Old Man in which Brooks made jokes about events in world history. Sandler recalled that his father loved listening to Brooks do that routine.

Stan Sandler also introduced Adam to the movies of the Marx Brothers. They were five Jewish brothers who made very successful movies in the 1920s and 1930s. The Marx Brothers' movies starred anywhere from three to all five brothers. They were filled with slapstick pranks and silly one-liners, and are still seen as classic comedy. In the days before videotapes and DVDs, Stan and Adam watched Stan's favorite Marx Brothers movies whenever they were aired on television. One time Stan woke Adam up at one o'clock in the morning because a Marx Brothers movie was starting.

Adam said about his father, "He was twenty when he started having a family, and he was always the coolest dad. He did everything for his kids, and he never made us feel like he was pressured. I know that it must be a great feeling to be a guy like that."[10]

Adam also learned at an early age that it felt good to do nice things for others. At the age of seven he sang the song

"The Candy Man" for patients in a Manchester nursing home. "The Candy Man" was the theme song from the 1971 movie *Willy Wonka and the Chocolate Factory*. It was based on the book *Charlie and the Chocolate Factory* by Roald Dahl and was the first movie version of the book.

Like most boys, Adam loved to play sports in his spare time. Bill Dow remembers, "We played basketball. We

Adam Sandler's Little League baseball team.
Sandler is in the bottom row, second from the left.

played football. Adam was always a good athlete. He was a very good baseball player. But he was a very slow runner. His running was hilarious. His arms were going a mile a minute but his legs were going so slowly."[11]

Adam did fairly well in school until he entered middle school. He recalled, "Until sixth grade, I really did well in school. All of a sudden, I said, 'I can't read and be so serious in class anymore.' I don't know why, but I just started to have fun."[12]

Around the same time, he started to like girls. He thought having a good sense of humor might not be enough. The way to a girl's heart, he felt, was to be a rock musician. So he started taking lessons at the respected Berklee School of Music, fifty miles south of Manchester in Boston.

On many occasions, Adam's friends would climb inside Judy Sandler's car before she drove Adam to Boston. They would then sit and wait inside the Berklee school office during Adam's lesson. Then the boys and Adam's mother would spend the rest of the day in the city visiting places such as the Museum of Science or the New England Aquarium.

Dow almost had a second home at the Sandler house, where he learned about the Sandlers' Jewish background. Dow said, "His parents were very nice, very outgoing. I used to call his mother, 'Mom.' I found Mr. Sandler to be very funny. But he was a big, tough guy so you couldn't take him on.

"We had lots of friends with different backgrounds. The Sandlers certainly introduced me to Jewish heritage in a lot of ways. But they didn't try to influence me in any way. He'd have me over to his house for the [religious] holidays. We'd play dreidel in his house. (The dreidel is a

226 Mrs. Clancy

Sandler's seventh-grade class photo, from Hillside Junior High School, class of 1978–1979. Sandler is in the front row, second from the left.

top people spin as part of a game played at Chanukah.)
We'd play basketball at the Jewish Community Center."[13]

Another childhood friend, Kyle McDonough, said,
"Adam was the go-to guy, the guy people liked to be
around. We had a close group of friends, six or seven guys.
We used to love being at his house. We'd play pool, Ping-
Pong. His parents were the most down-to-earth people,
caring and loving. They incorporated his friends into the
family."[14]

McDonough, a Catholic, recalled, "The first time I
ever had matzo ball soup was at his house."[15] Matzo ball
soup is a traditional Jewish dish.

There was a significant minority of Jewish students
at Hillside Junior High School. Bill Dow says he went
to "probably about two dozen bar mitzvahs" in middle
school.[16] Still, Adam often had to deal with bigoted
comments from other kids.

Dow remembered, "He used to fight kids. Rodney
Hanks called him [an offensive name for a Jew]. The two of
them didn't get along. Adam flipped out and drilled him.
He [Adam] said, 'I don't take that, so I decked him.'"[17]

If Adam and his friends were not playing sports, they
were often at the movies. One popular movie released in
1980 when Adam was in junior high school was a comedy
titled *Caddyshack*. It was about the antics taking place at a
country club for wealthy people.

The movie received mixed reviews from the critics. One publication, *TV Guide,* said *Caddyshack* was "a slapstick comedy featuring a host of great clowns."[18]

One of the stars is Adam's boyhood hero, Rodney Dangerfield, who plays an annoying millionaire. *TV Guide*'s review said that Dangerfield's "opening scenes are some of the funniest on film."[19]

Other stars of *Caddyshack* are *Saturday Night Live* former cast members Bill Murray and Chevy Chase. Chase was one of the first big names on *Saturday Night Live*. He became famous for doing a slapstick pratfall.

Sandler and a girl classmate (above) were voted most popular students in the eighth grade by their classmates.

Kyle McDonough said, "We saw *Caddyshack* maybe twenty times. We memorized all the lines and quoted them all. When it came out we were just the right age for it."[20] Sandler has said *Caddyshack* was the biggest influence on his comedy.[21]

In the fall of 1981, Sandler entered Manchester Central High School. Adam did not excel like his older siblings had. But he was not a poor student. His junior-year history teacher Mike Clemons said, "He was full of mischief. He was an underachiever, like Bart Simpson. He was brilliant. He could have been valedictorian if he had applied himself. He always pulled a B in my class, but he could have been an A student."[22]

Adam loved playing the class clown. Whether or not he was disciplined depended on the teacher involved. Bill Dow recalled, "I was in Spanish class with him in all four of my years. He used to give one of our teachers, Miss Maclean, a hard time. He'd look up words in his Spanish-English dictionary and blurt out things in Spanish like, 'You're such a beautiful teacher,' but not grammatically correct. He was very unpredictable. Miss Maclean was very timid and passive, but an experienced teacher."[23] When a student acted out too much, she would put her foot down.

Adam's guidance counselor Bob Schiavone also remembered Adam as a student who would push the faculty. Schiavone recalled one incident when Adam was assigned to a punishment called internal suspension. As part of an internal suspension, students spent the entire school day in detention hall. They were not allowed to talk, eat, or socialize in any way. Schiavone said:

During Adam's high school years, Central had an assistant principal by the name of Ms. [Isabel] Pellerin. She was about five foot, two inches tall but tough as nails. The students hated to go to her office for punishment. One day Ms. Pellerin assigned Adam to internal suspension for his behavior. Adam went to internal suspension with a pillow, blanket, and a small portable TV. When he arrived in the room, he plugged in the

As a high school senior in 1984, Sandler (second from the left) was voted one of the school's four "class clowns" by his classmates.

TV. The internal suspension teacher contacted Ms. Pellerin, who was extremely angry at Adam at this time. She removed Adam from internal suspension directly to her office.

I heard about this incident and immediately went to Ms. Pellerin's office to see if I could somehow intervene on Adam's behalf, as I had tried to do on many other occasions. When I arrived at Ms. Pellerin's office, Adam was sitting in the outer office. He told me that he just got externally suspended from school and Ms. Pellerin was calling his parents to come and get him. I went in to see Ms. Pellerin hoping to get her to reduce that punishment. Ms. Pellerin accused me of always trying to take Adam's side and always trying to get him out of trouble. She was tired of Adam and, quite frankly, tired of me. She said to me that Adam was suspended and so was I. As Adam and I proceeded to go to my office, I was telling him how angry I was at him for being externally suspended. He said, "Well, Mr. S. you were suspended too."[24]

Actually, Bob Schiavone was not suspended. Isabel Pellerin did not have the authority to fire a guidance counselor. Schiavone added, "Ms. Pellerin was shooting from the hip, as she did quite often. As time went by,

I was in Ms. Pellerin's office many times trying to advocate for students. We had a kind of love/hate relationship. In an unusual twist, this was probably the one incident that really made Adam feel that I was on his side."[25]

Mike Clemons said: "I used to play off him and he used to play off me. He was not malicious, just funny. On one occasion I was teaching about Reconstruction and we were discussing the Lincoln assassination. He raised his hand and said Lincoln was the first Jewish president. I said there has never been a Jewish president. He answered that yes there was and it was Lincoln. I told him he was wrong and we went back and forth. Then he pointed to

Sandler (No. 40, front row) and the high school basketball team in his sophomore year, 1981–1982.

the textbook and said, 'It says right here that Lincoln was shot in the temple.' It was brilliant."[26]

Many of his classmates laughed alongside him. But not all. Some found his disruptions disturbing. Clemons said, "Chrissy Allen was a classmate. She teaches phys ed at the school today. She told him to shut up and let me talk so she could take notes."[27]

Bill Dow said Adam's attitude extended beyond the classroom. According to Dow, "He loved to do the Chevy Chase fall in the cafeteria. He would do a fake trip over

Sandler (top left) was also among those selected for having the "best hair" in his senior class in high school in 1984.

a chair and fall and the food went everywhere. A teacher would see it and say, 'Okay—Detention!' He [Sandler] tried to talk his way out of it and got argumentative. He'd say, 'What for? I fell down.' After a while teachers caught on so he would try to come up with more ways to pull antics."[28]

Sandler took part in some extracurricular activities. He was a skinny kid with frizzy hair, but was good enough to play on the junior varsity baseball and basketball teams. After school he liked shooting hoops with his friends at the Manchester Boys Club. It was located not far from the school. Clemons said, "That was the place to be to go play basketball. Adam wanted to compete but was always a wannabe athlete."[29]

Adam did manage to serve a short stint on the student council, but spent a lot of his time outside of classes with Manchester Central's drama club. It was called The Masquers. The guitar lessons also paid off as Adam played in a rock band. They performed at school dances and assemblies.

Adam's guitar playing apparently had no effect on one girl he especially liked. She was a dark-haired beauty named Linda St. Martin. Linda worked part-time as a model and dated older boys. Because Linda's and Adam's names were close alphabetically, they were always in the same homeroom.

"Adam would go up to her and ask her, 'When will you go out with me?' knowing she was out of his league."[30] Mike Clemons says, "She would answer, 'When Hell freezes over.' Adam would say to her, 'You won't go out with me because I'm Jewish.' She answered, 'I wouldn't like you no matter what you are.' I wonder if she regrets saying that now."[31]

Bob Schiavone says that Adam would talk to him about Linda. Schiavone says, "He couldn't understand why she didn't like him as much. He was probably a little overbearing with her, the way adolescent boys can be."[32]

Bill Dow remembers that Adam dated a lot of girls. He used his sense of humor to win over his dates. However, he never dated any of them seriously. Most were not Jewish. Dow says, "Religion was important to him. If the girls had been Jewish the relationships may have become more serious."[33]

As Adam's high school years were winding down, he had one serious issue on his mind. What would he do with the rest of his life?

Being Smitty and Stickpin Quinn

At the end of one's high school senior year, students usually vote for their fellow students who fit categories such as class brain, class jock, or class trouble-maker. These "honors" are often listed in the high school yearbook. Sandler was one of four students tied for the vote of class clown. Most people would not see that as training for a career.

But Adam Sandler was not like most people.

Whether clowning in the classroom or performing on the school auditorium stage, Adam loved entertaining. Show business, however, is a very difficult career to break into. Sandler's teacher Mike Clemons remembered, "Adam always said to me, 'I'm going to make a living in comedy.' I said, 'Adam, there are 5 million unemployed comedians in the United States now. Get real and get a profession.'" Clemons added, "How does that make me look now?"[1]

Sandler's guidance counselor Bob Schiavone was one faculty member who felt Sandler's goal was worth a shot. Schiavone said, "He always wanted to perform. What else could he do? He wasn't an athlete. He was a good musician; I remember him strumming his guitar. But he was not great. I didn't know what else he would do if he didn't do that. He looked at colleges [with good theater departments] like Syracuse and NYU (New York University)."[2]

Sandler was accepted at NYU and decided to attend college there. But first he wanted to see if he could make people laugh outside high school. Schiavone was not the only person to encourage him. When Adam asked his brother, Scott, what career path he should choose, Scott suggested that Adam follow his dreams.

Sandler said about his brother's advice, "If he hadn't said to do it, I wouldn't have thought it was a normal thing to do. I would have said, 'Mom and dad are going to get mad at me.' But because he told me to do it, and I knew that my parents respected his brain, I was like, he said to do it so it must be o.k."[3]

In the summer after he graduated high school, Adam decided to try comedy in a real nightclub. Nightclub audiences can range from people enjoying an evening out to sloppy drunks who torment entertainers. Known as hecklers, they get a thrill insulting comedians they do not consider funny. Many comedians learn to sharpen their skills by coming right back at hecklers with their own insults. Comedians also learn to be less sensitive to criticism by dealing with hecklers.

Adam Sandler began attending New York University in the fall of 1984.

The nearest city with a number of comedy nightclubs was Boston. Sandler learned that making a nightclub audience laugh was not as easy as cracking up his school classmates. He made his first stage appearance in the summer of 1984 at Stitches Comedy Club in Boston. Like many comedy clubs, Stitches had a weekly open mike night. That was the night when anyone could go onstage and try to make the audience laugh. Back at Manchester Central, Sandler could make kids laugh by popping his retainer in and out of his mouth. Unfortunately, in a city nightclub, that routine made Sandler look like an immature kid.

Sandler said, "I remember going on stage, not knowing what to say, hearing some drunk guy slurring, 'He's got a retainer.'"[4]

By late summer Sandler had moved into his dormitory at NYU. Unlike many colleges that have leafy quads and cozy campuses, NYU is located in an urban area of lower Manhattan called Greenwich Village.

Greenwich Village is filled with nightclubs and theaters. At night and on weekends, the streets are a mass of humanity. People come from other parts of New York City and its suburbs to enjoy the theater, the music clubs, the funky shops, and art galleries. Greenwich Village is as different from Manchester, New Hampshire, as Manchester is from Sandler's boyhood home of Brooklyn. By chance, Brooklyn is just across a bridge from Greenwich Village.

Sandler moved into a dormitory called Brittany Hall, filled with other freshmen. As NYU is different from most college campuses, Brittany Hall is hardly like most college dormitories. It is a fifteen-story-high brick structure that looks similar to numerous apartment buildings in the neighborhood. Although the campus and Sandler's dormitory were not typical, he and his friends acted like normal freshmen away from home for the first time. They put stereo speakers in their windows facing the street, and turned the volume high. Passersby could not help but hear the music of Led Zeppelin and other bands that Sandler and his friends blasted out their windows.

Sandler selected drama as his major, or major course of study. That means he would take more courses in drama than any other subject. Many of his classmates wanted to be serious actors. They often preferred foreign to American-made movies. To them, foreign movies were deeper than American movies and made audiences think. They saw American movies as brainless fluff filled with silly gags or car crashes.

Sandler was just the opposite. His main goal was not to send a deep message but to entertain audiences. Some teachers at NYU thought Adam was wasting his time in the drama department. One professor, Mel Gordon, said of Sandler, "He was terrible. A complete clown."[5]

Calling Sandler a clown was a backhanded compliment. He wanted to be a clown-like actor, like those in his favorite movie, *Caddyshack*. At night he took advantage of the location of his college. The best comedy clubs in New York were just a walk or cab ride away.

Actually, Sandler's first New York audience was in his own dormitory. Adam stood in front of the captive audience at Brittany Hall's coffee shop and zinged one-liners at them. He wrote some of his jokes himself. His roommate, Tim Herlihy, wrote some of Sandler's other jokes. Sometimes Sandler teamed up with other friends and they worked together as a comedy troupe. Sandler and his friends got laughs and applause from their audiences. However, most of their audiences were made up of college friends. Sandler wanted to see if he could make a crowd of strangers laugh.

As in high school, Sandler neglected his studies. But instead of horsing around in the classroom, Sandler tried to make being funny into an art. The cream of New York City's comedy nightclubs was the Comic Strip. Famous comedians such as Eddie Murphy, Jerry Seinfeld, Ray Romano, Jon Stewart, and Chris Rock started there. Sandler, just nineteen years old, talked himself into an audition.

Very few comedians are as lucky as Sandler was the day of his audition. Most receive rejection after rejection when trying out for comedy gigs. This is especially true at a nightclub like the Comic Strip. But something clicked when Sandler auditioned for Comic Strip talent coordinator Lucien Hold.

Hold said, "He was only nineteen years old and I signed him up immediately. He had all clean stuff—very quirky, very cute. I thought, this guy is really good. The next day I got a phone call from Adam thanking me for being so kind. For the longest time he would call me regularly, almost every day."[6]

Many talent coordinators such as Hold might find it annoying to have a newly discovered comedian—or anyone—calling almost every day. Sandler had such a pleasant and humble personality that he got away with it. He presented himself onstage the same way. Hold noted, "His jokes would bomb all the time, but he would never bomb. It was more about his own personality up there. He was so likable. And he got away with it."[7]

Even though Sandler was performing in one of New York City's top comedy nightclubs, he was still on the bottom rung of the comedian ladder. He made very little money. His total payment was about ten dollars a night.[8] Part of the payoff for performing at a place like the Comic Strip is exposure. Exposure means the possibility of being seen and discovered by more famous comedians and talent coordinators.

Of course, Sandler still had to eat, so he would do his best to find the least expensive restaurants in the city. To earn more money, Sandler took odd jobs. One was working behind the prescription counter in a pharmacy. Others included washing dishes and waiting on tables in restaurants. He also took his guitar and sang Beatles songs in the city's subway stations. He placed his opened guitar case on the ground in front of him and passersby tossed in coins or sometimes dollar bills.

While onstage, Sandler sometimes got nervous. And when he was nervous, he stuttered. A dormitory mate, Frank Coraci, joined Sandler's roommate Tim Herlihy to write jokes for Adam. Someone—possibly Sandler's brother, Scott—suggested that Sandler play his guitar onstage when he got nervous. That would give him something to hold onto. In addition, he could write funny songs to put in his act.

Some of the most successful comedians have used musical instruments as props. One of the funniest of the twentieth century, Jack Benny, used a violin. Current movie superstar Steve Martin began doing stand-up comedy with his banjo. There was no reason Sandler could not do the same with his guitar. To break up his joke telling, he strummed the guitar and sang a few silly songs. Before long Sandler was a regular at the Comic Strip.

All the while he was attending classes at NYU. However, his heart was in trying to build his comedy act. In fact, he seemed to be getting more out of his college years by meeting important people than learning in his classes.

One friend was a student named Lorenzo Quinn. Lorenzo's father was an award-winning actor named Anthony Quinn. Therefore, Lorenzo knew many show business people—including comedian and actor Bill Cosby. At the time, Cosby was starring in the hit television series *The Cosby Show*. Unlike most television programs, *The Cosby Show* was videotaped in New York City, not Los Angeles.

The Cosby Show was a half-hour-long situation comedy about the Huxtables, a successful African-American family living in Brooklyn. It also happened to be the number one most watched television show in the nation at that time.[9]

The Quinns introduced Sandler to Cosby as an up-and-coming young comedian. Sandler was given a chance most people can only dream about—an opportunity to audition for Bill Cosby. At first, it seemed that Sandler had turned this dream situation into a complete disaster.

In the late 1980s, several stand-up comedians were having success with foul-mouthed routines. The dirtier the jokes, it seemed, the bigger the success. But Bill Cosby became a megastar without resorting to garbage-mouth jokes. As Sandler launched into a routine filled with profanity, Cosby sat silently. His only advice for Sandler was to clean up his act. It seemed as though Sandler had blown it. Sandler went back to doing what he did best at the Comic Strip. In spite of the poor reception Sandler had from Cosby, Lucien Hold felt Sandler had a future on television. Another person who felt Sandler could make a career in comedy entertainment was Richie Tienken, one of the Comic Strip's owners. Tienken introduced Sandler to a talent manager named Barry Moss. By chance, Moss was also the casting director for *The Cosby Show*. Moss arranged for Sandler a second audition for Cosby.

Sandler was smart enough not to make the same mistake. He steered clear of dirty jokes and landed his first major acting role. Sandler was hired to play Smitty, a goofy friend of teenager Theo Huxtable, played by Malcolm-Jamal Warner. Sandler acted in only a few episodes. The first one aired on December 3, 1987. Sandler's biggest role aired on March 24, 1988. The episode title was "The Prom."

In that episode, Theo and Smitty are double-dating. At first they decide to impress their dates by renting a limousine. Then they decide that a helicopter would really impress their dates. Naturally, everything goes wrong. For example, the wind from the helicopter's rotors makes a mess of their dates' perfectly styled hairdos. At the end of the episode, Theo, Smitty, and their dates arrive at the prom after it had ended.

Warner said of Sandler's character, "Smitty was like the cool nerdy one in Theo's crew ... but then again Theo and his friends were all cool and nerdy!"[10]

Warner added, "Adam seemed to have his own kind of comedic style which was fun to watch, and really great to see him develop into what he's become famous for. I remember we'd hang out every now and then and go see Adam and [comedian] Chris Rock do stand up. As far as his character on the show and him as a person, Adam was very personable, funny, and well liked. Mr. Cosby obviously liked him. He kept bringing him back."[11]

Host Ken Ober and Colin Quinn are among those pictured here on the set of MTV's *Remote Control* in 1988. Adam Sandler had a recurring role on the game show—one of the earliest breaks in his career.

Sandler's friends back in Manchester could hardly believe their eyes when their old friend showed up on television. Kyle McDonough was astounded. He announced, "*The Cosby Show* was huge at the time. My friends were saying, 'Can you believe there is Adam on *The Cosby Show*?'"[12]

After Sandler's run on *The Cosby Show* had ended, his manager Barry Moss lined him up for a different kind of television job. He would be working for a fairly new cable television network: MTV: Music Television. At the time MTV had been on the air just six years.[13] While there are many types of shows on MTV today, that was not the case in 1987. MTV showed almost nonstop music videos. So Sandler was given a risky role.

His first MTV job was host of one of MTV's earliest live telecasts from spring break. He then got a supporting role on a quiz show titled *Remote Control*. It was hosted by Ken Ober, and it ran from 1987 into 1990. In true MTV fashion, the setting was Ober's fictional parents' basement.

Contestants sat on recliners. They were asked questions about topics such as television shows, musical groups, and advertising slogans. Grand prize-winners could go home with anything from a new car to a resort vacation.

While Ober was the host, the announcer and Ober's sidekick was comedian Colin Quinn. Sandler later joined the cast and played two roles. One was Quinn's fictional cousin, Stickpin Quinn. In the other role he played a popular young man who dated attractive female celebrities. As Sandler described the celebrity, the contestants had to decide who he was referring to. At one point *Remote Control* toured college campuses across the nation. Sandler was becoming a minor celebrity. When he walked through the streets of Greenwich Village, young people recognized him and said hi. Then he would go inside his dormitory and study for a test or write an essay.

Sandler appeared on one other MTV program. It was titled the *MTV Half-Hour Comedy Hour*. It consisted of thirty minutes of stand-up routines. Sandler was one of several comedians on the show. It was about this time that he met a young woman who worked in the cosmetics industry. Her name was Margaret Ruden, and before long they were dating.

New York City is the place to be for stand-up comedians or people who want a future in live theater or on Broadway. But for those who want to act in movies, Los Angeles is the place to be. In the late 1980s, Sandler put his college studies on hold and moved to Los Angeles.

As he did at the Comic Strip in New York City, Sandler performed stand-up at the hot Los Angeles comedy club The Improv. He met other struggling comedians, including a San Francisco native named Rob Schneider and a former Arizona resident, David Spade. Sandler also had his dream nearly come true. He had a major role in a movie titled *Going Overboard.* It takes place on a cruise ship. Sandler plays Shecky, a bartender who dreams of being a comedian.

The movie may have been set aboard a cruise ship, but in the eyes of moviegoers it was a shipwreck. It was not shown in theaters. It went straight to home video. One critic, Jason Coffman, wrote, "Now, I have found the worst film I have ever seen."[14] He also wrote, "If you're an Adam Sandler fan, stay away from this film. . . . This is a horrible, horrible movie."[15]

Sandler's movie career seemed stalled. It was back to doing stand-up at The Improv. But it was not long before he got the job as a writer for *Saturday Night Live.*

Cajun Man, Opera Man, and a Surprise Phone Call to a Sick Fan

Working for *Saturday Night Live* meant a move back to New York City in the fall of 1989. Adam had no problem making the three-thousand-mile move back across the country.

He also did not mind working hard. That was important since working on a live, weekly television program is a grind. The writers get together on Monday and brainstorm rough ideas for sketches for the coming week's show. Producer Lorne Michaels and his assistants listen to the ideas. Michaels and his staff scrap some ideas totally. They tell the writers to work on others that have potential.

Sandler said, "It helped my whole career when I went from a stand-up comedian who would write maybe a couple of jokes a week that I would be excited about to—I think I was twenty-three when I got on the show—all of a sudden writing a few skits a week and helping other guys out with their ideas and trying to do jokes for their skits."[1]

On Tuesday, Sandler and the other writers would firm up the ideas for sketches Michaels thought would work. Stagehands would start building sets for Saturday's show. By Wednesday the final sketches were chosen. Thursday was the day for polishing the final sketches. The writers edited and rewrote them constantly. If a particular sketch relied more on physical comedy than spoken jokes, the scene in which an actor fell after tripping over a chair might be adjusted by a few seconds. On Friday, the cast members rehearsed while the writers did last-minute rewriting. Saturday afternoon and evening were times for dress rehearsals.

Once the show went on the air live at 11:30 P.M. in New York, there was no room for mistakes. The show ended at 1:00 A.M. The cast members, writers, and other staffers often let off steam with after-show parties at some of the liveliest nightspots in New York. On Sunday, they all caught their breath. Then on Monday, it was back to work.

Chris Rock was one of the regular cast members at the time. He often played the role of an angry African-

American man named Nat X. On one show, Rock, in character as Nat X, read a list titled "Top Five Reasons Why Black Guys Don't Play Hockey." Rock remembered, "Adam actually gave me the best joke I ever had on the show."[2] The number one reason on the list was "'Don't feel the need to dominate another sport'. . . Adam gave me the joke. Adam Sandler! Adam Sandler, man. Good guy."[3]

Sandler hit the big time December 8, 1990. On that night Sandler made his first appearance on *Saturday Night Live*. Actor Tom Hanks was the guest host. One sketch called for a character born in Israel. Sandler announced that he can do an Israeli accent. Sandler only had two lines, but this was live television and he was intensely nervous.

Just before the young man from New Hampshire was about to make his national television debut, he said to Hanks, "'Hoo, I'm nervous,' and he [Hanks] goes, 'Hey, it's going to be all right.' I said, 'Man, I feel like I'm going to faint or something.' He [Hanks] goes, 'Well, don't.'"[4]

Sandler delivered his two lines perfectly. However, it was awhile before he was able to go on the air without feeling butterflies in his stomach. For a long time he would repeat his lines right up until airtime.

Once actors in the *SNL* cast become well known, they develop characters that show up in frequent sketches. In the late 1990s, Will Ferrell and Cheri Oteri played high school cheerleaders in many episodes. In the early 2000s, Rachel Dratch played Debbie Downer, who always found a way to ruin a good time. These characters are often based on people everyone meets in his or her life. Who has not met someone like Dratch's character Debbie Downer who always has something depressing to say?

The first attempt to find a recurring character for Sandler was a total failure. It was in mid-February 1991 and the first Iraq war had just broken out. One way to get a nation to support a war is a method called propaganda— portraying the people they are fighting as completely evil. The *SNL* staff came up with an evil character named Iraqi Pete. Sandler was selected to play him.

The problem was that Iraqi Pete came off as so hateful that television viewers found the character repulsive. NBC received so much negative mail that Iraqi Pete was dropped and never seen again.

Like most television programs on commercial networks such as NBC, *Saturday Night Live* does not air new shows in summer. Instead, they air reruns from the previous season. Sandler kept very busy during this off-season. He finally graduated from New York University. He also had a part playing a clown in a movie that was combination comedy and tragedy. It was the story of an alcoholic clown, titled *Shakes the Clown*. The movie was not a hit and received mixed reviews from film critics.

When summer turned into fall of 1991 and new *Saturday Night Live* episodes were telecast, Sandler took over the show like a rocket. He was one of a group of young

The 1992 cast of *Saturday Night Live*: Chris Farley, Al Franken and Melanie Hutsell (front row, left to right); Chris Rock, Julia Sweeney, Dana Carvey and Rob Schneider (middle row, left to right); Adam Sandler, David Spade, Ellen Cleghorne, Kevin Nealon, Phil Hartman and Tim Meadows (back row, left to right).

cast members being groomed to replace others who had been around for several years. Almost right away Sandler came up with a winning recurring character. About halfway through every *Saturday Night Live* telecast a cast member hosts "Weekend Update," a satirical look at the past week's news. In fall 1991, cast member Kevin Nealon was the anchorperson for "Weekend Update." Sometimes other cast members play special correspondents who interact with the anchorperson.

In the fall of 1991, Sandler came up with a character he called simply the Cajun Man. He wore a straw hat, overalls, and red suspenders over a flannel shirt. He looked like the stereotype of a Cajun, or person of Cajun (French Canadian) descent from south-central Louisiana. He spoke in a thick Cajun accent, putting the accent on the last syllable of each word. Instead of pronouncing train "station" as "stay-shun," Sandler would say "stay-shone."

A typical conversation, with Kevin Nealon in the role of anchorperson and Adam Sandler as the Cajun Man, went like this:

> **Kevin Nealon:** Now that the Mardi Gras is over, the next big celebration for American partygoers is spring break. Here to talk about his recent trip to Daytona Beach is our own party correspondent, the Cajun Man.

> **Cajun Man:** Hey, Kev-own.

Adam Sandler appears as "Cajun Man" alongside Kevin Nealon during a "Weekend Update" segment of *Saturday Night Live* in 1994.

Kevin Nealon: I understand you go to Daytona Beach every year, don't you?

Cajun Man: Tradi-shone.

Kevin Nealon: And you look like you got some color there, too?

Cajun Man: Suntan lo-shone.

Kevin Nealon: Okay, Cajun Man. You've been down on the beach a lot. How's your body looking?

Cajun Man (flexes an arm): Defini--shone.

Kevin Nealon: How do you stay so thin?

Cajun Man: Metaboli-soam.

Kevin Nealon (asking doubtfully): Cajun Man?

Cajun Man (sheepishly): Liposuc-shone.

Kevin Nealon: That's what I thought."[5]

Sandler said he developed the idea for the Cajun Man in a very basic way: by observing people. He was in a New York City restaurant and a visitor from Louisiana with a thick Cajun accent kept telling the maitre d' that he had a "reserva-shone."

Sandler developed another character by observation. While walking through New York, he often passed a street musician who sang opera for tips. Like Sandler used to do in the subway with his guitar, this man put out a cup for people to toss in money. Sandler's character became known as Opera Man. He appeared on camera in a full-length black wig, full cape, and a bow tie. He sang about current news events in an operatic style. As in Italian, every word seemed to end in a vowel. His lines were funny. On top of that, the sketch gave Sandler a chance to show off his singing voice.

In one sketch, a photograph of then President George H. W. Bush was shown in the background. President Bush appeared to be sleeping. Opera Man started singing in a very quiet voice, "Shh, el doze-o. Shh, el doze-o." Then he suddenly sang loudly, "El inferno, violencia, armageddon!" as photos of violent actions were shown in the background. Then, the same photo of Bush sleeping was shown. Opera Man ended as he began, singing softly, "Shh, el doze-o. No disturbe presidante."[6] The joke was that President Bush was ignoring world crises as if he was sleeping through them.

Not all of Sandler's recurring characters appeared as part of "Weekend Update." He also played Canteen Boy, based on some kids he knew in Manchester. He said, "Canteen Boy is just the boys I knew, kids when I was growing up in the neighborhood. . . . He's just a silly kid who stayed in the Scouts too long."[7]

The *SNL* staff discovered that with his vocal talents, Sandler did a fine job impersonating rock stars. Whenever a sketch called for a parody of a particular singer, Sandler was the person for the job. At different times he impersonated Bruce Springsteen, Axl Rose, and Bono.

Sandler even had a recurring role as a teenage girl. Her name was Lucy, and she worked at the Gap clothing store with two other girls named Cindy and Christy. Cindy and Christy were also played by men. Cindy was played by Chris Farley and Christy was portrayed by David Spade. The act was a satire on teenage clothing store workers who care more about gossiping than helping customers. The fact that men were playing the girls' roles made the skits hilarious.

Although he played silly roles, Sandler was serious about his comedy. When an audience did not laugh, he took it personally. He said, "When I get nothing from a crowd, I get so upset that it bruises me for a week. When I do something wrong, it ruins me until the next show."[8]

After the 1991–1992 season ended, Sandler took some time to explore more work outside television. He had a minor role in a movie titled *Coneheads*. It was about a family of aliens who literally had cone-shaped heads. The Coneheads were a recurring sketch from *SNL*'s very early days in the 1970s. While the movie was filmed in the summer of 1992, it was not released until 1993. Not surprisingly, a movie based on a television sketch almost twenty years old did not do well.

Meanwhile, Sandler continued his stint as a cast member on *Saturday Night Live* the next season. One character he played every October was a Halloween costume expert. He gave advice on ways to make Halloween costumes using household items such as paper bags or geometry tools like protractors. Of course, the cheap costumes looked ridiculous, but Sandler's Halloween costume expert swore they would look great when kids went out trick-or-treating.

It was also early in 1993 that Sandler decided to record a comedy record album. He titled it *They're All Gonna Laugh at You.* Most of the cuts were spoken word routines, but there were some songs. Sandler had performed two of them on earlier *SNL* episodes. One was a silly number about Thanksgiving. Another was a tribute to the cafeteria workers at his high school. It was titled "Lunch Lady Land," and it described a woman cafeteria worker who had to wear a hair net because her hair was falling out.

Sandler's old friend Kyle McDonough said, "Oh, yeah. The lunch lady was definitely taken from the Central High lunch ladies, not any one in particular, but the lunch ladies in general at Manchester Central. Or every lunch lady in the country."[9]

They're All Gonna Laugh at You was nominated for a Grammy Award for best comedy album. It was also awarded a platinum record.[10] That means it sold over one million copies in the United States.

Sandler spent the summer of 1993 making two movies. One was titled *Airheads*. It is about a lame heavy metal band that takes over a radio station in order to force the disc jockey to play the band's demo tape. The other movie was *Mixed Nuts*. It was written by noted screenwriter Nora Ephron. She has written successful movies such as *Sleepless in Seattle, When Harry Met Sally,* and *Silkwood. Mixed Nuts* takes place on Christmas Eve at an emergency phone center. Sandler plays a young man who lives downstairs from the phone center.

Two women who were big fans of Sandler in real life were college roommates in Boston. One was Kelly Kerrigan from Sandler's hometown of Manchester. Her father Bob Kerrigan was a friend of Sandler's former guidance counselor Bob Schiavone. Kelly's roommate was named Clare.

During the summer of 1993, Clare went back to her hometown of Jacksonville, Florida. One night Clare was attacked in her house. She was shot and stabbed several times. While Clare was in the hospital recovering, Kelly's parents got in touch with Bob Schiavone. Perhaps Schiavone could get Sandler to call Clare and cheer her up.

It was a long shot. Sandler by then was a very busy man and like all famous people, he gets special requests all the time.

One day the phone rang in Clare's hospital room. Kelly Kerrigan recalls:

> Clare answered it and the person on the other line was Adam's agent. He told her he had Adam Sandler on the line for her. She didn't believe it. But as he started talking to her she recognized his voice. She was so excited. She kept telling him how great he was. He said, "No, you're the one who is great. You've made it through all this." They were both just complimenting each other. She was just amazed that he called. He was funny, too. It sounded like a friend calling a friend. He was making her laugh. He sounded very genuine.[11]

Sandler told Clare to call him when she returned to Boston. He would get tickets for her and Kelly to see *Saturday Night Live* in New York. When she got back to college, Clare called Sandler. As promised, he returned her call and offered to get her tickets. Unfortunately, scheduling conflicts prevented them from actually getting together for a live show. However, the incident shows Adam Sandler's true nature.

While Sandler was now one of *SNL*'s stars, the show was getting poor reviews and low ratings. Critics said it was not as funny as it had been in previous years. They tended not to blame the actors. Several writers had left before the 1993 season. Critics called it "Saturday Night Dead." But by then Sandler had his following. His loyal viewers loved his loony songs and his recurring characters

Adam Sandler performs "The Chanukah Song" during his return to *Saturday Night Live* as host on November 16, 2002.

such as Lucy the Gap clerk, Opera Man, the Cajun Man, and Canteen Boy.

Airheads and *Mixed Nuts* were both released in 1994. Neither movie was successful. It seemed that if Sandler was to have a hit movie he would have to write it himself. Sandler looked up his old college roommate Tim Herlihy.

Herlihy and Sandler had taken different career paths. Herlihy entered law school and was working as a lawyer in New York City. Sandler convinced Herlihy to leave the courtroom and start writing jokes. Herlihy tried out as a staff writer on *SNL* and passed the audition.

While Herlihy and Sandler worked on *SNL* together, they also tackled another project: a movie screenplay. Unlike Sandler's other movies, in this one he would be the lead character. They spent much of the summer of 1994 shooting their new movie *Billy Madison*.

But Sandler had one more season at *Saturday Night Live*. It was during this last season that he became known for one of his biggest contributions to the show. It was during the holiday season and Sandler was about to sing one of his silly songs on "Weekend Update." Norm Macdonald had replaced Kevin Nealon as the anchorperson. Macdonald introduced Sandler, who was about to play guitar and sing a Chanukah song he wrote. The song was dedicated to Jewish children like himself who often feel lost around Christmas. The lyrics are mainly names of famous Jewish people who many did not know were Jewish. The lyrics are funny and the song received good-natured laughs.

On one occasion in 1994, comedian Damon Wayans was the guest host. Wayans and Sandler got along so well that Sandler asked Wayans, "Why don't we do a movie? We should do an action movie together."[12] In the business world such conversations are often spoken but later forgotten.

By the winter of 1995, Sandler had had enough of *Saturday Night Live*. Some say the show had had enough of him as well. There are television historians who say Sandler was fired in order to bring in a fresher cast. However, Sandler said being on the show was great. But by then he felt "like I [had] started repeating myself. I didn't want to do that. I wanted to get into growing as much as I can."[13]

It was time to tackle the movie industry.

The Fans vs. the Critics

Some might say the story line of *Billy Madison* was similar to that of Sandler's life. It was basically the tale of a slacker who never grew up—and never wanted to grow up—until he had to. He got through life doing the bare minimum.

Sandler once said, "If I would be out of school for a day, I'd watch *Love Boat* reruns and then *Family Feud* and stuff. I'd be so excited I'd fake sick for the rest of the week."[1]

However, there were major differences in the lives of Adam Sandler the actor and Billy Madison the character. Adam was not from a wealthy home while Billy's father is a billionaire. Adam may not have tried his hardest in school, but he graduated from one grade to the next on his own merits. Adam also got good, if not great, grades. Billy graduated not because he deserved it. He advanced from one grade to the next because his father paid school officials to do so.

Billy is used to living a life of ease at his father's expense. Yet Billy is in for a shock when his father retires. Billy expects to be chosen to run the business and rake in the cash. But Billy soon learns that a greedy and undeserving employee named Eric Gordon will inherit his father's business.

Billy wants to prove that he is worthy of owning his father's company. He tells his father he will do anything to earn his father's trust—even if it means repeating every school grade from kindergarten through high school. In addition, Billy promises to do it in twenty-four weeks. When Billy attends the earliest grades, he is a grown man in classes with six- and seven-year-old children. In one early scene, Billy seems to forget how much stronger he is than the children. So during recess he powerfully throws a dodge ball at a smaller, weaker kid. Thankfully, the child is not severely hurt.

In time, Billy shows the young children that he understands what they are going through. He has been there before. So he helps them through difficult situations.

The role was perfect for Sandler. He said, "Billy's the closest I've come to playing myself. I feel so much pressure because I want it to be as good as it can be."[2]

Sandler might have looked on-screen as if he was just being lazy. In reality, making a movie is hard work. Actors work as many as sixteen hours a day.

Sandler not only had pressure of memorizing lines and being convincing. In many movies, independent screenwriters compose the script while actors interpret the writers' work. In the case of *Billy Madison*, Sandler and Tim Herlihy wrote the script. They were responsible for tweaking each line of dialogue and bit of action until they felt it was perfect.

Sandler's former teacher Mike Clemons remembered, "When Adam was promoting *Billy Madison*, he came back here [to Central High School]. A lot of the girls were going gaga over him. He was single and in his twenties. He told me he named a character after me in the movie. I asked who it was and he said you'll have to see the movie. I won't tell you."[3]

Clemons saw the movie. He learned that the character named Mr. Clemons is a crusty, old man on whom Billy and his friends play a practical joke. The real Mr. Clemons got a good laugh from it.[4]

The movie was a financial hit. It was meant to appeal to teenagers and college students. And they loved it.

Professional movie critics mostly agreed on one thing about *Billy Madison*. Nearly all of them hated it. One critic, Chris Hicks, wrote: "In small doses, Sandler can be charming and funny, as demonstrated by some 'Saturday Night Live' skits and the laughs he got in a pair of otherwise forgettable comedies from last year, *Airheads* and *Mixed Nuts*. But here, completely unrestrained and on-screen for nearly the entire film, Sandler is just gratingly obnoxious."[5]

Adam Sandler in a scene from *Billy Madison* (1995).

Despite what critics said, Sandler knew how to reach his audience. Sandler's performance was nominated for—but did not win—an MTV Movie Award for best comedic performance. While the MTV Movie Awards are big with MTV's teenage audience, most movie critics do not take them seriously.

Sandler's next movie was titled *Happy Gilmore*. But while Sandler was involving himself with *Happy Gilmore*, he was also thinking about the conversation he had had a year earlier with Damon Wayans on the set of *Saturday Night Live*. Sandler kept his word about making a movie with Wayans. He spent the little free time he had working with two screenwriters named Joe Gayton and Lewis Colick. Gayton and Colick wrote a movie titled *Bulletproof* to star Sandler and Wayans.

Wayans recalled, "A year later, he [Sandler] sent me the *Bulletproof* script and it was incredible."[6]

There was a major change in Sandler's personal life in 1995, too. He and his girlfriend Margaret Ruden were becoming very serious. Some reporters said that he had proposed to her. Others even claimed they had a wedding planned for September 1995 and had sent out wedding invitations. Then, for some reason, the two suddenly split up.

Sandler is a private man who does not like to talk about his personal life. So what really happened between him and Ruden is not known. However, many feel the breakup had to do with their careers. When they met, Sandler was a struggling comedian and Ruden was just starting out in the cosmetics industry.

About six years had since passed. Sandler was now a big-name movie actor and Ruden was a cosmetics executive. His career brought him to Los Angeles. Her career led her to New York. Being three thousand miles apart was hard for them. It is believed by many that the distance led to their breakup.

With his famous name and fun personality, he did not have trouble finding other women to date. For a while he and actress Alicia Silverstone were seeing each other.

In 1996, *Happy Gilmore* was released. Sandler plays Gilmore, a young man who wants to be a hockey player. There is just one problem—he cannot skate. One day at a golf driving range he realizes he can hit a golf ball with incredible power. Still, he would rather play hockey than golf.

Sandler's boyhood friend Kyle McDonough was the inspiration for *Happy Gilmore*.[7] Kyle's wife, Jill McDonough, said, "Kyle was a hockey player who could hit a golf ball a mile. But he doesn't have that kind of mean temper and he doesn't wrestle alligators."[8]

Jill added that as part of an extra feature on one of the *Happy Gilmore* DVDs, Sandler thanks Kyle for inspiring the main character.[9]

In the movie, Happy Gilmore learns his grandmother needs money to save her house. To earn money he becomes a professional golfer. Some funny events take place as Gilmore tries to succeed in the gentlemanly sport of golf with his background in the rough world of hockey.

Movie critics had mixed reactions to *Happy Gilmore* when it was released in February 1996. Those who tended to like serious movies and dislike slapstick gave it bad reviews. They felt that Sandler thought all he had to do was act goofy and people would be entertained.

Brian Lowry, critic for *Variety*, a publication geared toward members of the entertainment business, wrote, "Sandler remains a thoroughly grating onscreen personality with zero acting range."[10]

On the other hand, some critics enjoyed *Happy Gilmore*. They were not looking for a movie with a serious message. Their attitude was if a comedy makes them laugh, then it works. One critic, Phil Villarreal, said it was better than Sandler's favorite comedy, *Caddyshack*. Villarreal wrote, "From beginning to end, there's not a slow moment in *Happy Gilmore*, the Tiger Woods of gleefully idiotic comedy. For many, *Caddyshack* is the ultimate duffer jokefest. Even though that 1980 film is hilarious, it's not even funny enough to carry 'Happy Gilmore's' clubs. Sandler is one of the finest comic talents ever to grace the screen."[11]

Sandler also recorded a second comedy album released in summer 1996. It was titled *What the Hell Happened to Me?* Like his first album, *They're All Gonna Laugh at You,* this one combined both comedy routines and funny songs. This album also included Sandler's now famous "The Chanukah Song."

During that summer Sandler and a group of friends toured the United States in a rock and roll band he called the Goat Band. With Sandler singing and playing guitar, he and his friends performed both songs from his albums and rock classics. When he played "Lunch Lady Land," his costar from *Saturday Night Live* Chris Farley dressed up like a high school lunch lady and danced around the stage. Farley was very overweight. The sight of him dancing and dressed like a cafeteria lunch lady brought the crowds to roars of laughter.

The movie *Bulletproof* was released in September 1996. Unfortunately, the mixed reaction from movie reviewers for *Happy Gilmore* was not the same for *Bulletproof.* There were all the things one would expect in an action/comedy: chase scenes, shootings, crashes, fights, juvenile jokes, and filthy language. Sandler's costar Damon Wayans says the movie gives the viewers a serious question to mull over: "Where do you draw the line between friendship and doing your job?"[12]

The movie begins with Wayans and Sandler as partners in crime. Sandler plays a small-time car thief named Archie

Moses. Early in the movie viewers realize that Wayans is not a real criminal but a police officer doing undercover work. Archie feels betrayed. The plot becomes complicated as Wayans's character, Rock Keats, needs Archie's help as he tries to arrest a powerful drug lord.

Most critics disliked the movie. Typical was the review by critics Mick Martin and Marsha Porter. They said, "The two [characters] squabble and survive with only a few bright comic moments in this generally mean-spirited mess."[13]

Surprisingly, "The Chanukah Song" from Sandler's second album took on a life of its own. Instead of just being one of several tracks on the album, the song received a lot of airplay on radio stations. Around the holiday season, listeners called their local stations to request it. It became as popular on radio stations in December as traditional Christmas carols.

Isabel Pellerin, the assistant principal at Manchester Central High School, said after Sandler became famous, "I can't believe he's making all that money for things he was being punished for here. I thought he would grow up. Instead he grew rich."[14]

Early in 1997, Sandler began work on a new movie. It would be a new genre, or style of movie, for Sandler: a romantic comedy titled *The Wedding Singer.* Despite his movies' negative reviews, movie studios were willing to take chances with Sandler for one reason. People went to see his movies and they all made money.

Billy Madison brought in roughly $26 million dollars in ticket sales. *Happy* Gilmore made about $38 million. Even the poorly reviewed movie, *Bulletproof,* took in $22 million.[15] It seemed like everything Sandler touched was magic. In 1997, his second album, *What the Hell Happened to Me?* went platinum. Like his first album, it was also nominated for a Grammy Award in the best spoken comedy category. Right away he released a third album titled *What's Your Name?*, which was all songs.

However, life was not all rosy for Sandler at this point in his life. On December 18, 1997, Sandler's close friend and former *SNL* costar Chris Farley was found dead in his apartment in Chicago. Doctors said that he had died from abusing alcohol and illegal drugs cocaine and heroin. Farley was just thirty-three years old.

Suddenly Adam Sandler—the man who loved making people laugh—could not stop being depressed.[16] Two months after Farley's death, Sandler said, "I have never gone through this before. I had grandparents pass away, and that hurts a lot. But that's natural. This is an unnatural death. And I can't stop thinking about it."[17]

Sandler tried laughing through his tears. He concentrated on his memories of his friend. In February 1998, he said of Farley, "I like thinking of him. I like

Adam Sandler and Chris Farley in an *SNL* sketch from 1994. After Farley's untimely death, Sandler became a major supporter of the Chris Farley Foundation.

smiling. I like thinking that he's listening and I like still trying to make him laugh."[18]

Sandler was about to be cast in a movie titled *Very Bad Things*. It is a dark comedy about a murder. But Sandler never appeared in it. There are different versions why. One is that he could not fit it into his filming schedule. Another is that he was so depressed over Farley's death that he did not want to make a morbid movie.

Not long afterward, Farley's brother, Tom Farley, Jr., and other members of the Farley family founded the Chris Farley Foundation. The foundation works with young people to deliver messages about the dangers of substance abuse. It uses humor to get its messages across. A foundation statement reads, "Whenever we can, we communicate the way Chris would have—with humor!"[19] It seems only natural that Sandler has played a major role working with the Chris Farley Foundation. That included appearing in a video to support the foundation.

Sandler's movie *The Wedding Singer* is a feel-good movie. Some said it was Sandler's first movie that boys would feel comfortable taking a date to. Sandler's friend Tim Herlihy was the sole scriptwriter and his NYU friend Frank Coraci was the director.

The movie takes place in the 1980s. The setting is used to poke fun at the fads and styles of that decade. This includes big, puffy hairdos; Rubik's Cubes; and break dancing. Sandler plays Robbie Hart, a truly nice guy who used to sing in a rock band. When the band never becomes big, he starts singing at people's weddings to earn money. His fiancée of six years liked Robbie when he was a rock singer. But to her, a wedding singer's job is a loser's job. She jilts him on his wedding day. He is brokenhearted. Movie critic Phil Villarreal raved, "Sandler proves here that he's not only a brilliant comedian, but a talented actor."[20]

Not everybody liked the movie. Famous film critic Roger Ebert blasted Sandler's acting ability. Ebert wrote, "The basic miscalculation in Adam Sandler's career plan is to ever play the lead. He is not a lead. He is the best friend, or the creep, or the loser boyfriend. He doesn't have the voice to play a lead."[21]

Like Sandler's other movies, *The Wedding Singer* pulled in theatergoers. The movie made about $80 million.[22]

For his performance in *The Wedding Singer*, Sandler was nominated for some minor awards. He won in the category "favorite actor in a comedy movie" in the Blockbuster Entertainment Awards. They were given by Blockbuster, the video and DVD rental company. However, the Blockbuster Entertainment Awards are now defunct. He was also nominated for an American Comedy Award for funniest actor in a leading role in a movie. The American Comedy Awards are defunct as well.

Sandler's next two movies, *The Waterboy* and *Big Daddy,* were throwbacks to his first movies. They reminded people of *Billy Madison* and *Happy Gilmore*. In

Sandler and Drew Barrymore in a scene from *The Wedding Singer* (1998).

The Waterboy, Sandler combined his *Saturday Night Live* characters the Cajun Man and Canteen Boy to create a character named Billy Boucher. Billy is a misfit water boy at a Louisiana college who proves himself on the football field. In *Big Daddy,* Sandler plays a single man named Sonny Koufax who refuses to grow up. His character is similar to *Billy Madison.* Instead of going to school all over again like Madison did, Sonny adopts a young son and becomes a responsible man and a good father.

Around that time, Sandler went to a party and met a pretty brunette named Jackie Titone. Titone worked as an actress and a model, but was not famous like Sandler. She is also eight years younger. Sandler asked Titone on a date and she turned him down. But he was persistent, and soon they were dating. Sandler joked on David Letterman's late night television show, "When she was five years old and learning to read I was thirteen and learning to read."[23]

Jackie had a small part in *Big Daddy.* She plays a waitress who serves the young boy Sonny adopts. That was her first appearance in a feature film.[24]

Again, both movies made money. *The Waterboy* earned about $161 million and *Big Daddy* took in approximately $163 million.[25]

When one critic, Philip Martin, reviewed *The Waterboy,* he basically said all Adam Sandler movies are the same. Martin wrote, "Look, it's an Adam Sandler movie, OK? It's supposed to be stupid. . . . Adam Sandler movies are like

Henry Winkler and Adam Sandler in a scene from *The Waterboy* (1998).

kumquats—you either like them or you don't. It doesn't matter what anybody has to say about the kumquat, the kumquat just isn't going to change its nature."[26]

A friend who produces several of Sandler's movies is Jack Giarraputo. He said, "We all know what it's like to be a bit of a loser. I think our movies give our kids hope."[27] Regardless of movie critics' opinions, by the end of the 1990s Sandler was a financial success. He was getting paid nearly $20 million per movie.[28]

Despite his wealth, Sandler does not show off. He does not live a typical Hollywood lifestyle. He still likes to eat at the same type of places where he ate as a teenager in Manchester. In 1999, he took a trip back to his hometown. Sandler said, "I was in New Hampshire with my family at a pizza place. The kid working there goes, 'Hey, you look like Adam Sandler.' I said, 'Yeah, I know.' He goes, 'What's your name?' I go, 'Adam Sandler.' And he goes, 'Whoa, that's a coincidence.'"[29]

A Stellar Performance from Opera Man

One would think people would praise Sandler for not getting caught up in the glamour scene of the movie industry. Indeed, many people do. They find his attitude refreshing. He does not spend a lot of money on designer clothes just to show off.

Yet even his choice to live a casual lifestyle gets criticized.

In 1999, *People* magazine—one of the most read magazines in the country—put Sandler on the list of the top ten worst-dressed people in the entertainment business. A fashion model named Roshumba Williams compared his dress style to that of a slacker teenager. She said, "He looks like he eats Cap'n Crunch cereal and channel-surfs all day in his underwear and a T-shirt."[1]

One fashion critic, Pamela Keogh, said that Sandler puts on an act by dressing as he does. Keogh remarked that by dressing down Sandler is telling the public, "Yes, I get millions a picture but I am a regular kind of guy."[2]

However, his old school friend Bill Dow says, "Adam was never into suits. He was always into comfort clothes. He never really liked getting dressed up. He was probably asked one time why he dresses down and he probably answered, 'This is how I dress.'"[3]

The cover of Sandler's next compact disc, *Stan and Judy's Kid,* is a photograph showing Sandler in his typical wardrobe. The CD, released in 1999, shows Sandler wearing a sweatshirt, white wrinkled pants with one pant leg raised too high, and black sneakers. Some said the highlight of the compact disc was "Chanukah Song Part II." It is to the tune of the first Chanukah song, but with new lyrics about different Jewish celebrities. *Stan and Judy's Kid* was nominated for but did not win a Grammy for best spoken comedy album.

In July 1999, Sandler showed just how seriously he takes the movie industry. He made a major business decision by starting his own production company. He titled it Happy Madison Productions, combining the names of two of his early movies. As head of a movie production company,

Sandler is involved in the behind-the-scenes actions as well as acting.

The producer has probably the most important job in making a movie. He or she chooses which movies are to be made. Then the producer has to raise the money to make the movie. That runs well into the millions of dollars. The producer hires the crew that will make the movie, such as a director and the actors. It also means hiring stagehands, stunt people, make-up artists, and costume designers. The producer is in charge of making sure the movie is well publicized and advertised in advance. One must know a lot about both business and the movie industry to be a producer. Sandler was taking on a big responsibility by starting his own production company.

Happy Madison would be producing Sandler's own movies. The first movie produced by Happy Madison was a comedy starring Sandler's friend and former *Saturday Night Live* costar comedian Rob Schneider. The second film produced by Happy Madison was a comedy starring Sandler titled *Little Nicky*.

As he did so many times before, Sandler plays a geeky character. In *Little Nicky,* he plays the youngest son of Satan. Nicky is a nerdy little fellow who tries to stop his two bully brothers from spreading Hell on Earth. Unlike some of Sandler's earlier comedies, the reviews of *Little Nicky* were nearly all bad. One critic, Charles Taylor,

Adam Sandler in *Little Nicky*. The film was the second movie produced by Sandler's Happy Madison Productions.

wrote, "The movie doesn't have one genuine moment of imagination, good timing or comic inspiration."[4]

On September 11, 2001, an event took place in the United States that made movies and comedy compact discs suddenly seem very unimportant. Nearly three thousand people were killed in a series of terrorist attacks that hit four locations. Muslim radicals belonging to a terrorist group known as al Qaeda ("the base" in Arabic) hijacked four commercial airplanes. They crashed one into the Pentagon, the building housing the headquarters of the United States Defense Department. Hundreds were killed there. Another was supposedly headed to Washington, D.C., when passengers fought back. The plane crashed in an isolated field in Pennsylvania and all the passengers were killed.

Most of the casualties were committed by hijackers who flew two airplanes into two skyscrapers in New York City. The buildings were over a hundred stories high and among the tallest in the world. The two towers were part of a complex called the World Trade Center. Well over two thousand people died at the scene of the World Trade Center. Several hundred were firefighters who had gone there to rescue people.

The reaction from across the world was shock and horror. People everywhere sent aid to help the survivors. Americans were united in a way they had not been for decades. It did not matter if one was a Democrat or

Republican. It seemed like every American wanted to do something to help out. The entertainment industry went into high gear to assist those who needed help.

Just ten days after the attacks, an event called *America: A Tribute to Heroes* was held. Many celebrities appeared onstage to sing or offer a speech. *America: A Tribute to Heroes* was shown commercial free on numerous television networks. Average Americans made phone calls to donate money to help out survivors and relatives of victims. Some celebrities did not show their faces on-screen, but helped by answering phones and taking caller donations. These included Ben Stiller, Penelope Cruz, Brad Pitt, and Whoopi Goldberg—and Adam Sandler. Over $200 million was raised from the live show.[5]

Then, on October 20, 2001, a similar event was staged. This was a marathon Concert for New York City. It lasted five and a half hours. One purpose was to raise money to aid survivors and victims' families. Another purpose was to honor the memory of those who died or were injured in the attacks. A third was to honor rescue workers, including members of the New York Fire Department and New York Police Department. Many from both departments were in the audience to hear the music live.

Some of rock music's biggest names performed at the Concert for New York City. Among them were David Bowie, Billy Joel, The Who, Mick Jagger and Keith

Adam Sandler in costume as "Opera Man." Sandler appeared as the character during the concert event, *Concert for New York City*, which was produced in the wake of the terrorist attacks on September 11, 2001.

Richards of the Rolling Stones, Paul McCartney of the Beatles, Bon Jovi, Elton John, and Destiny's Child.

Then, in the middle of these classic acts' performances, who should be introduced but Adam Sandler in character as Opera Man. With his cape, black wig, and bow tie, Opera Man sang a tribute to New York City lasting five minutes and twenty-two seconds. Nearly the first two minutes was a praise to New York City Mayor Rudy Giuliani. Of course, Sandler sang some funny lines. He also sang tributes to the New York Yankees and the musicians who performed at the concert.

He urged tourists to visit the city. Since it was so soon after the attacks, some people thought New York was a dangerous place to visit. But the biggest laughs came when Opera Man ridiculed Osama bin Laden, the Saudi Arabian leader of al Qaeda.[6]

He received as much applause as the famous rock groups who performed that night. Over $30 million was raised by the concert.[7]

Americans did not allow themselves to forget the terror and heroes of September 11, 2001. But in time they went back to their routines. Sandler's next movie was titled *Punch-Drunk Love*. Anyone entering a movie theater expecting to see a typically silly Adam Sandler comedy was in for a big surprise. Sandler plays a man named Barry Egan. Egan is a lonely businessman who becomes the victim of a blackmailing scheme. *Punch-Drunk Love*

Emily Watson and Adam Sandler in a scene from *Punch Drunk Love* (2002). The film marked Sandler's first attempt at a more serious, dramatic role.

is considered a romantic comedy. While there are some funny moments, *Punch-Drunk Love* is also a very serious film. It is an artistic film, and a very mature film. Some may call it dark, or sullen.

Punch-Drunk Love was directed by Paul Thomas Anderson, whose work is known for being offbeat. Critic Jess Cagle wrote, "As far as romantic comedies go, it's very strange, which is what you would expect from director Paul Thomas Anderson. . . . What you don't expect is an art film starring Sandler, whose lowbrow comedies have earned nearly $400 million since 1998 and have made him an idol of teenage boys, a cult figure on college campuses and a punch line for dismissive film critics."[8]

Sandler's acting performance earned him what many consider his first serious award nomination: a Golden Globe nomination for best actor in a motion picture musical or comedy. The Golden Globes are a project of the Hollywood Foreign Press Association. That is a group of journalists who cover the movie industry for publications outside North America. They are taken very seriously by the movie industry.

Sandler did not win. The winner in Sandler's category was Richard Gere for his role in the movie musical *Chicago*. But by being nominated by such an admired group, Sandler earned something else: respect for his talent as an actor.

The good feelings movie reviewers had toward Sandler's performance in *Punch-Drunk Love* did not carry over to his next movies. He played the lead in 2002 in a remake of a classic old movie. The original movie was titled *Mr. Deeds Goes to Town*. It was released in 1936 and starred legendary Gary Cooper. The director, Frank Capra, was also a legend in the movie industry. It is a comedy about a well-meaning and humble man who inherits a fortune.

Sandler's version was simply titled *Mr. Deeds*. Actors and directors always take a risk when remaking a classic movie. Much of the time they fail. Critics mostly hated *Mr. Deeds*. Many did not like Sandler adding his typical gross-out humor to a classic movie from a more innocent time. Others thought Sandler had a lot of nerve trying to step into the shoes of movie heroes Gary Cooper and Frank Capra.

Still, *Mr. Deeds* was a money-maker. It earned $126 million in the United States and $170 worldwide.[9]

Jeff Fisher, the head of distribution and marketing for Sony Studios, which released *Mr. Deeds*, had words for the critics. Fisher said, "Adam took a bit of a beating from the press for taking on a Frank Capra film, but this shows just how much audiences love him."[10]

In 2002, Sandler also founded his own animation company. He called it Meatball Animation, named after his pet bulldog. He used Meatball Animation to make his first feature cartoon, *Eight Crazy Nights*. The title is from a line in Sandler's "The Chanukah Song." In fact, he used the animated movie to introduce a third version of the song.

There are mentions of Christmas in *Eight Crazy Nights,* but the main story line is about a Jewish man who is a modern-day version of Ebenezer Scrooge. In this case, the main character, Davey Stone, has no use for Chanukah. The animated Davey looks much like Sandler. Sandler's girlfriend, Jackie Titone, does the voice of Davey's girlfriend.

Sandler had hoped the movie would become an annual tradition for holiday season viewing.[11] He told MTV, "The intention was to write a funny movie and hope that maybe every year you get to see it somewhere."[12] One of Sandler's co-writers, Brooks Arthur, said, "It's a great way to introduce the holiday to people who know nothing about Jews."[13]

Unfortunately, it was not to be. Critics found the movie offensive and the story dull. Some said the character of Davey was not sympathetic. The many bathroom jokes seem out of place for a holiday-themed movie. Worst of all, the movie did not make the amount of money hoped for. It earned $23 million.[14] That may seem like a lot, but it is small compared to Sandler's other comedies.

Sandler seemed to take the "win some, lose some" attitude about his movies in stride. In 2003, he costarred with Jack Nicholson, one of the most popular actors of all time. The movie was a comedy titled *Anger Management.*

Sandler plays a man who gets treatment for an anger problem. Nicholson plays his counselor. One of the funniest scenes takes place when Nicholson and Sandler together sing the song "I Feel Pretty" from the musical *West Side Story*.

Critics' reviews, again, were mixed. Those who did not like Sandler's style of movie disliked *Anger Management*. However, others thought Sandler and Nicholson played off each other perfectly. Critic Stella Papamichael from the esteemed British Broadcasting Company (BBC) loved the movie. She wrote, "The pairing of Nicholson and Sandler is golden."[15] She also glowed, "Sandler's soft-centered charm is the key in bringing warmth to this otherwise wicked comedy."[16] *Anger Management* was also a smash with audiences. It earned nearly $134 million.[17]

At the same time *Anger Management* was filling theaters, Sandler had a special moment in his private life. On June 22, 2003, he and longtime girlfriend Jackie Titone were married in Malibu, California. They took their wedding vows on an estate overlooking the Pacific Ocean. Sandler dressed his bulldog, Meatball, in a tuxedo for the event.

His pride in his Jewish heritage was evident. The wedding ceremony was a traditional Jewish one. Jackie, who was not born a Jew, converted to Judaism.[18]

Sandler did not forget his boyhood friends from Manchester. Kyle McDonough was one who attended the happy occasion. McDonough said, "He brought out so many friends from here. He brought all of us out there and put us up. The food was spectacular. The setting was second to none. We saw so many stars there, [like] Dustin Hoffman, Henry Winkler, Rodney Dangerfield."[19]

A Man Who Likes to Give

Adam and Jackie Sandler settled into Sandler's three-story house overlooking the ocean in Malibu. By this time, Sandler was earning more than $20 million a movie.[1] He clearly needs no more material things in his life. So he has decided to give away much of his money.

He had already helped many charities such as the Chris Farley Foundation and groups that aided victims of the 9-11 terrorist attacks. One other group he has aided is the Epidermolysis Bullosa Medical Research Foundation (EBMRF). Epidermolysis bullosa (EB) is actually a group of diseases that affects one's skin. Most who have EB are children, and they have trouble healing from minor scrapes or cuts. Instead of healing, they get sores and blisters. Some cases are mild. However, others are severe and even life threatening. It is estimated that as many as one hundred thousand Americans suffer from some form of EB.[2]

Sandler took part in a fund-raiser for EB sufferers called the CelEBration on the Pier in Santa Monica, California. Santa Monica Pier is the site of a midway with carnival games. A total of $150,000 was raised.[3]

Sandler is also one of a handful of celebrities who hand drew greeting cards to raise money to find a cure for EB. Actor Reese Witherspoon drew on her card multicolored balloons and the words "Happy Birthday." Supermodel Heidi Klum drew a butterfly surrounded by hearts. Sander drew on his card the face of a bulldog. Surrounding it are paw prints and the words, "Thanks for thinking of me. I was sad."[4]

One other charity in which Sandler has taken an active part is the Life Rolls On Foundation (LRO). LRO raises money to help people with spinal cord injuries. At one LRO event, Sandler took part in an auction as part of a prize. The highest bidder got a chance to surf with Sandler and Jesse Billauer. Billauer is a Southern California surfer who became paralyzed in a surfing accident in 1996. People said he would never surf again. However, he has been able to return to surfing by adapting his equipment and techniques. The winner of the auction prize was reality

Adam Sandler with his wife, Jackie, and daughter, Sadie, at the fundraising event "CelEBration on the Pier" on Saturday, September 29, 2007.

television star and heiress Paris Hilton. She paid $17,500 for the chance to surf with Sandler and Billauer.[5]

When he is not involved in charity work, Sandler is usually at the movie studio. He made two movies in 2004. In one, he teamed up with Drew Barrymore, his costar from *The Wedding Singer*. The duo starred in another romantic comedy. This one was titled *50 First Dates*. Sandler plays Henry Roth, who falls in love with a girl named Lucy Whitmore.

Lucy was in an auto accident several months before the movie begins. As a result, she suffers severe memory loss. Every morning she wakes up forgetting everything that happened in her life since the accident. Yet Henry is so in love with Lucy that he spends every day making her fall in love with him again. *50 First Dates* was released on Valentine's Day weekend 2004.

One critic, Eleanor Ringel Gillespie, loved *50 First Dates*. She wrote, "There's something in Drew Barrymore that brings out the best in Adam Sandler, and there's something in him that brings out the best in her. *50 First Dates* is an almost perfect Valentine's movie. Like the stars' last collaboration, *The Wedding Singer,* it's charmingly romantic and funny (think chick flick). And, like so many of Sandler's lowest-common-denominator comedies, it's suffused with slapstick and gross-out gags (think very-guy Sandler fan)."[6]

On the other hand, critic Kevin Thomas of the *Los Angeles Times* wrote, "It's only February, but the abysmal *50 First Dates* will be hard to beat as the worst movie of the year."[7]

So once again, an Adam Sandler movie received mixed reviews from the critics.

50 First Dates turned out to be a bigger hit than *The Wedding Singer*. While *The Wedding Singer* earned roughly $80 million, *50 First Dates* pulled in over $120 million.[8]

50 First Dates is a movie with a happy ending. However, there was a sad event in Sandler's real life around the time the movie was filmed. His father, Stanley, died of cancer in 2003. Sandler paid tribute to his father with a special dedication presented at the end of *50 First Dates*. It read, "This movie is dedicated to Stanley Sandler, my father, my mentor, my teacher, my coach, my idol, my hero, my family's leader, my mom's best friend, and by far the coolest guy I will have ever known. We will miss you every day, but we will always try to make you proud."[9]

Sandler's other 2004 movie was another attempt to play a semi-serious role. It is titled *Spanglish,* as in a combination of Spanish and English. The story is about an immigrant maid from Mexico named Flor. Flor moves to the United States to make a better life for herself and her young daughter. She gets a job as a live-in maid at the summer home of John and Deborah Clasky. John is played by Sandler while Deborah is portrayed by Tea Leoni. The theme is the importance of family as Flor and her daughter adjust to life in a new country.

Like *Punch-Drunk Love, Spanglish* is a movie where Sandler could not be his usual silly self. The director, James L. Brooks, said of Sandler's role, "He had some very tough scenes."[10]

Although it had been five years since Sandler's last compact disc, he came out with a new one in 2004. It was titled *Shhh...Don't Tell*. It was similar to his previous CDs in that it was filled with skits and songs. But this time he hosted a wide variety of guest performers. These included former and then current *Saturday Night Live* cast members David Spade, Maya Rudolph, and Molly Shannon. It also included a memorial tribute to his father.

In 2005, Sandler tried his luck at remaking another classic movie, *The Longest Yard*. It was originally released in 1974 and starred a ruggedly handsome actor named Burt Reynolds. Reynolds plays a disgraced former NFL football player now in prison. He organizes a football team of fellow convicts to play against a team of mean guards organized by a corrupt warden. In the remake, Sandler plays Reynolds's role.

Again, those who like Sandler gave the movie high marks. Those who do not like Sandler were brutal. In her review of *The Longest Yard*, Leah Rozen of *People* magazine wrote of Sandler, "Rarely has such a hypercharged Hollywood career been built on so minor a talent."[11]

Chris Rock, Burt Reynolds, and Adam Sandler (left to right) in the 2005 remake of *The Longest Yard*.

Comments like those have caused Sandler to rarely give interviews to newspapers and magazines. Comedian Chris Rock, who costars in *The Longest Yard*, defended Sandler. Rock stated, "The press didn't really give him any respect. . . . Everybody dissed him, and it's like, 'Now you want me to talk to you?' If I were him, I wouldn't talk either."[12]

In May 2006, Sandler and his wife Jackie had their first child, a daughter named Sadie. Typically, Sandler did not tell the print media. Instead, he announced it on his Web site.

In June, Sandler's next movie, *Click,* was released. *Click* is a comedy-drama about a married father of two children who works too hard and ignores his family. Sandler's character, Michael Newman, is given a magic remote control by a strange man. The remote lets him stop time and go years into his past or future. *Click* is a touching movie about a man who learns to work less hard and appreciate his family.

Many fans and critics compared it to a movie called *It's a Wonderful Life,* often shown during the holiday season. Many also said it was like a modern-day version of Charles Dickens's *A Christmas Carol.* Some movie reviewers criticized *Click* for being too close to those other movies. As usual, others said the movie would have been better if Sandler did not put childish gross-out jokes in it. But like most of his other movies, *Click* made a lot of money: over $137 million.[13]

Halfway around the world that summer, the nation of Israel was involved in a thirty-four-day war with the neighboring country of Lebanon. Many Israeli civilians were injured and their houses were damaged by rockets fired from Lebanon. Sandler donated four hundred Sony PlayStations to Israeli children who had been hiding in bomb shelters during missile attacks.[14] Some people criticized him. They felt he should help by rebuilding houses or aiding injured people. But Sandler responded that he donated the PlayStations to "bring happiness to their [the children's] hearts."[15]

That December he did a similar deed for a teenage brother and sister in his hometown of Manchester. Both Stephanie Hudon, age fifteen, and her eighteen-year-old brother, Kevin, were suffering from cancer. Sandler arranged to have a PlayStation 3 filled with games sent to the Hudons. He also sent autographed DVDs, shirts, and a poster from *The Longest Yard* to them.

By now Sandler seemed to be using his character of Michael Newman of *Click* as a personal role model. When his daughter, Sadie, was just over a year old, a fan asked him via the Internet, "How has fatherhood changed your life?"[16] Sandler answered, "It has been great. All your priorities change. I definitely work a lot less."[17]

There soon was another addition to the Sandler household. After the death of their pet bulldog, Meatball, the Sandlers adopted another bulldog. They named her Matzoball, after the common Jewish food.

Sandler proved again in 2007 that he could put the goofiness aside when his movie *Reign Over Me* was released. His role was his most serious to date. Sandler plays Charlie Fineman, a New York City dentist whose wife and three daughters die in the terrorist attacks of September 11, 2001.

After their deaths he has a breakdown. He quits his dental practice and refuses to talk about his family. He travels through the city on a motorized scooter. Throughout the movie he looks scruffy, with a beard and shaggy, uncombed hair.

By chance, Charlie meets up with his former college roommate, Alan Johnson, played by Don Cheadle. Alan has a successful dental practice. He is married and has two small children. At first Charlie acts as if he does not remember Alan. In time, Alan tries to help Charlie cope with the tragedy in his life. Through his newfound friendship with Charlie, Alan realizes he is unhappy with his marriage and dental practice. The two men bond together in an unusual friendship.

For one of the few times, both Sandler and his movie received more positive than negative reviews. Several critics commended Sandler's performance. Jack Mathews of the widely read *New York Daily News* gushed, "Cheadle is good, as always, but Sandler's portrayal of a guy on the perennial brink of a psychotic breakdown is amazing."[18]

Paul Arendt of the British Broadcasting Company wrote, "The central performances are subtle and intelligent—Sandler especially is a knockout."[19]

Unfortunately, *Reign Over Me* did not earn as much money as Sandler's comedies. It made a little over $19.6 million.[20] And while *Reign Over Me* received mostly good reviews, it was not nominated for any major awards.

His next movies were more standard Sandler fare. One was titled *I Now Pronounce You Chuck and Larry*. Sandler and Kevin James play two straight firefighters who pretend to be gay. While they cannot get legally married, they can be declared a "domestic partnership." That way one character can get needed insurance benefits he could not get if single. The majority of reviews were terrible. But not surprisingly for a Sandler comedy, *I Now Pronounce You Chuck and Larry* made a ton of money—over $119 million.[21]

His follow-up film, *You Don't Mess With the Zohan,* features as a setting an unlikely subject for a comedy: the ongoing conflict between the Israelis and the Palestinians. Sandler plays Zohan Dvir, an Israeli special agent who is tired of the dangerous situations he encounters every day. He fakes his death and sneaks off to the United States where he takes an unusual job for someone with his background—a hairstylist. The critics were kinder to *You*

Don't Mess With the Zohan than for *I Now Pronounce You Chuck and Larry*. But again, the majority were negative. Yet Sandler fans do not care what critics say. *You Don't Mess With the Zohan* cost $90 million to make but earned over $201 million.[22]

That just means Sandler has more wealth to share. His co-star in *Reign Over Me*, Don Cheadle, is one founder of a group called Ante Up for Africa. The other founders are professional poker player Annie Duke and a friend of theirs named Norman Epstein.

As the organization's name implies, the group plays poker to help raise funds to help people living in a terrible situation in Africa. For several years, a civil war has been raging in a region called Darfur in the nation of Sudan. One result has been the ethnic cleansing of black Africans in Darfur at the hands of a Muslim government. According to the founders of Ante Up for Africa, this genocide has resulted in four hundred thousand deaths among the residents of Darfur.[23] Another 4 million Darfur residents have been displaced from their homes and live in wretched refugee camps.[24]

As part of his fund-raising activity for Ante Up for Africa, Sandler was one of several celebrities who took on professional poker players on July 2, 2007, in Las Vegas. It cost five thousand dollars for each contestant just to enter the tournament.[25] A total of seven hundred thousand dollars was raised for the victims of the crisis in Darfur.[26]

While Sandler helps people from across the globe, he has never forgotten his roots. In October 2007, he donated one million dollars to the Boys and Girls Club of Manchester, New Hampshire.[27] That is where he played basketball as a teenager. He announced his donation with a videotape. In the videotape, he recalls memories of playing basketball and Ping-Pong and—typical of Sandler—having a bathroom accident. Manchester's Boys and Girls Club serves three thousand young people.[28] When the Boys and Girls Club staff member Tracy Adams was asked to discuss Sandler's donation, she said that Sandler requested that they do not discuss it. Sandler wanted to give his donation without bragging.[29]

Early in 2008, Sandler broke his foot in a sports injury. But he managed to arrive on crutches for yet another charity function. This organization is called Autism Speaks. Autism is a condition that affects one's brain. People with autism tend to live in their own worlds. They cannot understand their own feelings and often act out.

Autism Speaks has several purposes. One is to fund education programs that help autistic children. Another is to donate money for research to help find prevention and treatment for autism. A third is to raise awareness of autism and its effects on others.

The cable television station Comedy Central hosted a gala fund-raiser on April 13, 2008, for Autism Speaks. Similar events have had titles such as *The Night of One*

Hundred Stars, or *The Night of Two Hundred Stars.* This one was humorously called *Night of Too Many Stars.*

Sandler's role was the subject of a celebrity roast. In a celebrity roast, a famous person is honored by his friends or fellow entertainers. They insult the person, but it is all in good fun and the subject knows it. But in this case Sandler acted insulted when jokes were made at his expense.

During the celebrity roast, Comedian host Jon Stewart told Sandler he rated his movie *I Now Pronounce You Chuck and Larry* two thumbs up. Stewart added, "I give it two thumbs up on a scale of one thousand thumbs."[30]

Instead of laughing along, Sandler acted insulted. Sander replied as part of a rehearsed act, "Wait a minute. Are you insulting me? What are you saying—one thousand thumbs? What does that mean?"[31]

Stewart answered, "It's a celebrity roast. We're supposed to give you a hard time. We don't mean it."[32]

Sandler replied, "Sorry about that. The foot's hurting."[33]

Then comedian and television host Conan O'Brien took the stage. He was a writer on *Saturday Night Live* when Sandler was a writer and cast member. O'Brien joked, "Adam was originally hired as a writer on *SNL*. His skits always stood out because they were the only ones written in crayon."[34]

In response, Sandler called the six-foot four-inch, red-haired O'Brien a "tall piece of red cabbage."[35]

Adam Sandler and Seth Rogen in a scene from *Funny People* (2009).

The evening was a success financially as well. Over $2.6 million were raised.[36]

However, Sandler showed that he was very capable of laughing at himself. He poked fun at his poor movie reviews. When a fan asked him if he was surprised to become a success in the movie business, Sandler sarcastically answered, "What surprised me was all the critical acclaim I received."[37]

On December 25, 2008, Sandler's movie *Bedtime Stories* was released. This family adventure is about a hotel janitor played by Sandler. He makes up bedtime stories and tells them to his niece and nephew while his sister is away for a job interview. Strangely, the stories become true. As is typical, most critics panned it while fans went to see it in hordes. *Bedtime Stories* earned much more than what it cost to make.[38] In 2009, Sandler starred in a movie called *Funny People*. It is a comedy-drama in which Sandler plays a comedian named George Simmons. Simmons is told by a doctor that he has a serious illness and a short time to live. When Simmons's health starts improving, it appears he will survive after all. He starts to examine more closely what is truly important in his life.

While many celebrities are in the news for substance abuse problems, marital issues, or brushes with the law, Sandler has had none of that. His former teacher Mike Clemons said of Sandler, "How many movie stars do you know who have never been involved in any kind of scandals with drugs or alcohol? He's only been married once."[39]

Sandler was once seriously asked if he is a comedian who acts or has he crossed the line to become an actor. He answered, "I was obsessed with comedy and I still am. But I went to college. I studied acting. It was on my mind, too, to become an actor. So I don't know what I am."[40]

There is one thing we do know—Adam Sandler is a very generous man.

Chronology

1966—Adam Richard Sandler born September 9 in Brooklyn, New York.

1971—Family moves to Manchester, New Hampshire.

1984—Starts doing stand-up comedy in Boston nightclub in summer; enters New York University in New York City in fall.

1985—Signs to do stand-up comedy at the Comic Strip in New York City.

1987–1988—Acts in episodes of *The Cosby Show* from December 3, 1987, to March 23, 1988.

late 1980s—Appears on *Remote Control* and other programs on cable network MTV.

1989—Moves to Los Angeles to try to make career in movies; first movie, *Going Overboard*, released; signs as writer for *Saturday Night Live*; moves back to New York City.

1990—First appearance on *Saturday Night Live* on December 8.

1991–1995—Regular cast member on *Saturday Night Live.*

1991—Appears in movie *Shakes the Clown;* graduates from New York University.

1993—Appears in movie Coneheads; releases first compact disc, They're All Gonna Laugh at You; surprises injured fan in hospital with unexpected phone call.

1994—Movies *Airheads* and *Mixed Nuts* released; introduces "The Chanukah Song" on *Saturday Night Live.*

1995—Moves permanently back to Los Angeles; first lead actor role in a movie, *Billy Madison.*

1996—Movies *Happy Gilmore* and *Bulletproof* released; second compact disc *What the Hell Happened to Me?* released; embarks on summer musical tour as leader of the Goat Band.

1997—Third compact disc, *What's Your Name?* released; close friend Chris Farley dies on December 18; eventually becomes involved in the anti-substance abuse Chris Farley Foundation.

1998—Movies *The Wedding Singer* and *The Waterboy* released; meets and begins dating actress/model Jackie Titone.

Chronology

1999—Fourth compact disc, *Stan and Judy's Kid*, released; begins own production company Happy Madison Productions; movie *Big Daddy* released.

2000—Movie *Little Nicky* released.

2001—Volunteers for *America: A Tribute to Heroes* on September 21; performs as character Opera Man in Concert for New York City on October 20.

2002—Movies *Mr. Deeds* and *Punch-Drunk Love* released; nomination for Golden Globe award for acting performance in *Punch-Drunk Love*; starts animation company, Meatball Animation; animated feature film *Eight Crazy Nights* released.

2003—Movie *Anger Management* released; Marries Jackie Titone on June 22; father Stan Sandler dies.

2004—Movies *50 First Dates* and *Spanglish* released; fifth compact disc, *Shhh . . . Don't Tell,* released.

mid-2000s—Does charity work for Epidermolysis Bullosa Medical Research Foundation and Life Rolls On Foundation.

2005—Movie *The Longest Yard* released.

2006—Movie *Click* released; Adam and Jackie have daughter, Sadie; donates PlayStations to Israeli children affected by Lebanon-Israeli War; donates PlayStation and autographed items to two children with cancer in Manchester, New Hampshire.

2007—Movies *Reign Over Me* and *I Now Pronounce You Chuck and Larry* released; takes part in Ante Up for Africa poker charity; donates one million dollars to Boys and Girls Club of Manchester, New Hampshire.

2008—Takes part in mock celebrity roast for *Night of Too Many Stars* for Autism Speaks; movies *You Don't Mess With the Zohan* and *Bedtime Stories* released.

2009—Movie *Funny People* released.

Filmography

1989 *Going Overboard*

1991 *Shakes the Clown*

1993 *Coneheads*

1994 *Airheads*

Mixed Nuts

1995 *Billy Madison*

1996 *Happy Gilmore*

Bulletproof

1998 *The Wedding Singer*

The Waterboy

1999 *Big Daddy*

2000 *Little Nicky*

2002 *Mr. Deeds*

Punch-Drunk Love

Eight Crazy Nights

2003 *Anger Management*

2004 *50 First Dates*

Spanglish

Adam Sandler

2005 *The Longest Yard*

2006 *Click*

2007 *Reign Over Me*

I Now Pronounce You Chuck and Larry

2008 *You Don't Mess With the Zohan*

Bedtime Stories

2009 *Funny People*

CDs

1993 *They're All Gonna Laugh at You!*

1996 *What the Hell Happened to Me?*

1997 *What's Your Name?*

1999 *Stan and Judy's Kid*

2004 *Shhh . . . Don't Tell*

Chapter Notes

Chapter 1.
Staring Into the Hotel
Room Mirror

1. Tom Shales and James Andrew Miller, *Live From New York* (Boston: Little, Brown and Company, 2002), p. 363.

2. Dave Stern, *Adam Sandler: An Unauthorized Biography* (Los Angeles: Renaissance Books, 2000), p. 60.

Chapter 2.
"He Was Full of Mischief,
He Was an Underachiever,
He Was Brilliant"

1. "Population Finder: King's County, New York," *U.S. Census Bureau,* n.d., <http://factfinder.census.gov/servlet/SAFFPopulation?_submenuId=population_0&_sse=on> (April 14, 2008).

2. "Population Finder: Manchester City, New Hampshire," *U.S. Census Bureau,* n.d., <http://factfinder.census.gov/servlet/SAFFPopulation?_submenuId=population_0&_sse=on> (April 14, 2008).

3. "Brooklyn Borough President Marty Markowitz Celebrates Jewish Heritage at Brooklyn Borough Hall," press release, *President of the Borough of Brooklyn,* April 26, 2004, <http://www.brooklyn-usa.org/Press/2004/apr26b.htm> (April 14, 2008).

4. Telephone interview with Bill Dow, March 24, 2008.

5. Ibid.

6. Ibid.

7. Associated Press, "Rodney Dangerfield Dead at 82," *MSNBC.com,* October 7, 2004, <http://www.msnbc.msn.com/id/6187136/> (March 28, 2008).

8. Ibid.

9. Ben Stiller, "Adam Sandler-comedian-Interview," *Interview,* December 1994, <http://findarticles.com/> (March 28, 2008).

10. Ibid.

11. Telephone interview with Bill Dow, March 24, 2008.

12. Bill Crawford, *America's Comedian: Adam Sandler* (New York: St. Martin's Griffin, 2000), p. 6.

13. Telephone interview with Bill Dow, March 24, 2008.

14. Telephone interview with Kyle McDonough, April 30, 2008.

15. Ibid.

16. Telephone interview with Bill Dow, March 24, 2008.

17. Ibid.

18. Review of *Caddyshack,* directed by Harold Ramis, *TV Guide.com,* n.d., <http://www.tvguide.com/movies/caddy-shack/review/126067> (April 3, 2008).

19. Ibid.

20. Telephone interview with Kyle McDonough, April 30, 2008.

21. Dave Stern, *Adam Sandler: An Unauthorized Biography* (Los Angeles: Renaissance Books, 2000), p. 27.

22. Telephone interview with Mike Clemons, March 7, 2008.

23. Telephone interview with Bill Dow, March 24, 2008.

24. Personal e-mail from Bob Schiavone, April 11, 2008.

25. Personal e-mail from Bob Schiavone, April 15, 2008.

26. Telephone interview with Mike Clemons, March 7, 2008.

27. Ibid.

28. Telephone interview with Bill Dow, March 24, 2008.

29. Telephone interview with Mike Clemons, March 7, 2008.

30. Ibid.; telephone interview with Bill Dow, March 24, 2008.

31. Telephone interview with Mike Clemons, March 7, 2008.

32. Telephone interview with Bob Schiavone, April 11, 2008.

33. Telephone interview with Bill Dow, March 24, 2008.

Chapter 3.

Being Smitty and
Stick Pin Quinn

1. Telephone interview with Mike Clemons, March 7, 2008.

2. Telephone interview with Bob Schiavone, April 11, 2008.

3. Ben Stiller, "Adam Sandler-comedian-Interview," *Interview,* December 1994, <http://findarticles.com/> (March 28, 2008).

4. "Sandler, Adam," *Current Biography Yearbook 1998* (New York: H. W. Wilson Company, 1998), p. 515.

5. Kendall Hamilton and Yahlin Chang, "Oh, You Silly Boy," *Newsweek,* November 9, 1998, <http://search.ebscohost.com/> (February 13, 2008).

6. Bill Crawford, *America's Comedian: Adam Sandler* (New York: St. Martin's Griffin, 2000), p. 19.

7. Betty Cortina, "Stop the Presses," *Entertainment Weekly,* June 18, 1999, <http://search.ebscohost.com/> (February 18, 2008).

8. Dave Stern, *Adam Sandler: An Unauthorized Biography* (Los Angeles: Renaissance Books, 2000), p. 49.

9. Tim Brooks and Earle March, *The Complete Directory to Prime Time Network and Cable TV Shows:*

1946–Present (New York: Ballantine Books, 2007), p. 1691.

10. Personal e-mail from Malcolm-Jamal Warner, April 25, 2008.

11. Ibid.

12. Telephone interview with Kyle McDonough, April 30, 2008.

13. Brooks and March, p. 828.

14. Jason Coffman, review of *Going Overboard,* directed by Valerie Breiman, *Bad Movie Night*, 2006, <http://www.hit-n-run.com/cgi/read_review.cgi?review=53387_coffman14> (April 26, 2008).

15. Ibid.

Chapter 4.

Cajun Man, Opera Man, and a Surprise Phone Call to a Sick Fan

1. Tom Shales and James Andrew Miller, *Live From New York* (Boston: Little, Brown and Company, 2002), p. 367.

2. Ibid., p. 364.

3. Ibid.

4. Ibid., p. 381.

5. "Saturday Night Live-Cajun Man-Video," (video clip), *NBC.com,* n.d., <http://www.nbc.com/Saturday_Night_Live/video/play.shtml?mea=2486> (April 29, 2008).

6. "Memorable Quotes for Saturday Night Live: The Best of Adam Sandler," *IMDB.com,* 1999, <http://www.imdb.com/title/tt0255573/quotes> (April 29, 2008).

7. Michael Cader, ed., *Saturday Night Live: The First Twenty Years* (New York: Houghton Mifflin, 1994), p. 23.

8. Ibid.

9. Telephone interview with Kyle McDonough, April 30, 2008.

10. Betty Cortina, "Stop the Presses," *Entertainment Weekly,* June 18, 1999, <http://search.ebscohost.com/> (February 18, 2008).

11. Telephone interview with Kelly Kerrigan, April 30, 2008.

12. "Production Notes," *Bulletproof,* DVD, directed by Ernest R. Dickerson (Universal City, Calif.: Universal Studios, 1996).

13. "Sandler, Adam," *Current Biography Yearbook 1998* (New York: The H . W. Wilson Company, 1998), p. 515.

Chapter 5.

The Fans vs. the Critics

1. "Face to Watch: Adam Sandler Saturday Night Live," *EW.com,* September 17, 1993, <http://www.ew.com/ew/article/0,,307997,00.html> (February 25, 2008).

2. "Adam Ribs," *EW.com,* February 17, 1995, <http://www.ew.com/ew/article/0,,296111,00.html> (February 25, 2008).

3. Telephone interview with Mike Clemons, March 7, 2008.

4. Ibid.

5. Chris Hicks, review of *Billy Madison,* directed by Tamra Davis, *Deseret News,* February 12, 1995, <http://deseretnews.com/movies/view/1,1257,190,00.html> (May 3, 2008)

6. "Production Notes," *Bulletproof,* DVD, directed by Ernest R. Dickerson (Universal City, Calif.: Universal Studios, 1996).

7. Telephone interview with Jill McDonough, May 7, 2008.

8. Ibid

9. Ibid.

10. Brian Lowry, review of *Happy Gilmore,* directed by Dennis Dugan, *Variety,* February 19, 1996, <http://www.variety.com/review/VE1117910802.html?categoryid=31&cs=1&p=0> (May 4, 2008).

11. Phil Villarreal, "ReView by Phil Villarreal: 'Happy Gilmore' Scores an Ace as a Golf Comedy," *Arizona Daily Star,* April 22, 2007, <http://www.azstarnet.com/accent/179384> (May 4, 2008).

12. "Production Notes," *Bulletproof,* DVD, directed by Ernest R. Dickerson (Universal City, Calif.: Universal Studios, 1996).

13. Mick Martin and Marsha Porter, *DVD and Video Guide 2007* (New York: Ballantine Books, 2007), p. 160.

14. Karen S. Schneider, "Last Laugh," *People,* November 30, 1998, <http://search.ebscohost.com/> (February 18, 2008).

15. "Assessing Sandler," *Daily Variety,* March 5, 2003, p. A6.

16. Janet Weeks, "For Adam Sandler, Moments Where His Heart Hurts a Little," *USA Today,* February 13, 1998, <http://pqasb.pqarchiver.com/USAToday/search.html?POE=Essentials> (May 6, 2008).

17. Ibid.

18. Ibid.

19. "What We Do," *The Chris Farley Foundation,* <http://www.thinklaughlive.com/752.html> (May 16, 2008).

20. Phil Villarreal, review of *The Wedding Singer,* directed by Frank Coraci, *Rotten Tomatoes,* August 2, 2002, <http://www.rottentomatoes.com/m/wedding_singer/articles/750249/sandler_proves_here_that_hes_not_only_a_brilliant_comedian_but_a_talented_actor> (May 6, 2008).

21. Roger Ebert, review of *The Wedding Singer,* directed by Frank Coraci, *RogerEbert.com,* February 13, 1998, <http://rogerebert.suntimes.com/apps/pbcs.dll/article?AID=/19980213/REVIEWS/802130303/1023> (May 6, 2008).

22. "Assessing Sandler."

23. Dave Stern, *Adam Sandler: An Unauthorized Biography* (Los Angeles: Renaissance Books, 2000), p. 186.

24. Ibid., p. 185.

25. "Assessing Sandler."

26. Philip Martin, review of *The Waterboy,* directed by Frank Coraci, *Arkansas Democrat-Gazette,* November 6, 1998, <http://www.ardemgaz.com/cgi/showreview .pl?The+Waterboy> (May 7, 2008).

27. Kendall Hamilton and Yahlin Chang, "Oh, You Silly Boy," *Newsweek,* November 9, 1998, <http://search.ebscohost. com/> (February 13, 2008).

28. Schneider.

29. "Sandler's Fame Game," *People.com,* April 12, 1999, <http://www.people.com/people/article/0,,615579,00 .html> (May 16, 2008).

Chapter 6.

A Stellar Performance from Opera Man

1. "10 Worst Dressed," *People,* September 20, 1999, p. 128, <http://www.people.com/people/archive/ article/0,,20129261,00.html> (May 15, 2009).

2. Ibid.

3. Telephone interview with Bill Dow, May 19, 2008.

4. Charles Taylor, review of *Little Nicky,* directed by Steven Brill, *Salon.com,* November 10, 2000, <http:// archive.salon.com/ent/movies/review/2000/11/10/ little_nicky/index.html> (May 20, 2008).

5. Michael Hastings, "America: A Tribute to Heroes: Synopsis," *All Movie Guide,* quoted on *Fandango.com,* 2008, <http://www.fandango.com/america:atributetoheroes_ v256429/summary> (May 20, 2008).

6. "Adam Sandler—Operaman at Concert for New York City (2002)," *YouTube.com,* August 16, 2006, <http://www. youtube.com/watch?v=ayzGlxHoTkk> (May 20, 2008).

7. "Concert for New York City Over $30 Million Raised," *VH1.com,* 2008, <http://www.vh1.com/news/features/ america_united/> (May 20, 2008).

8. Jess Cagle, "Sandler, Seriously," *Time Europe*, January 27, 2003, <http://search.ebscohost.com/> (May 19, 2008).

9. "Assessing Sandler," *Daily Variety,* March 5, 2003, p. A6.

10. Scott Bowles, "Adam Sandler, 'Mr. Deeds' Goes to Top of the Tox Office," *USA Today,* July 1, 2002, <http://search.ebscohost.com/> (February 13, 2008).

11. Naomi Pfefferman, "Crazy for Chanukah," *JewishJournal.com,* November 29, 2002, <http://www.jewishjournal.com/arts/article/crazy_for_chanukah_20021129/> (May 3, 2008).

12. Ibid.

13. Ibid.

14. "Assessing Sandler."

15. Stella Papamichael, review of *Anger Management,* directed by Peter Segal, *BBC.com,* June 5, 2003, <http://www.bbc.co.uk/films/2003/05/23/anger_management_2003_review.shtml> (May 23, 2008).

16. Ibid.

17. "Anger Management (2003)," *Rotten Tomatoes,* 2009, <http://www.rottentomatoes.com/ m/1121649-anger_management/?page=2&critic=columns&sortby=date&name_order=desc&view=#mo> (May 23, 2008).

18. Ulrica Wihlborg, "Adam Sandler, Wife Have a Baby," *People.com,* May 7, 2006, <http://www.people.com/people/article/0,,1191818,00.html> (February 22, 2008).

19. Telephone interview with Kyle McDonough, April 30, 2008.

Chapter 7.
A Man Who Likes to Give

1. "Men of the Week: Entertainment Adam Sandler," *Askmen.com,* 2009, <http://www.askmen.com/celebs/men/entertainment_60/95_adam_sandler.html> (October 18, 2007).

Chapter Notes

. . . .

2. "What Is Epidermolysis Bullosa (EB)?" *Epidermolysis Bullosa Medical Research Foundation,* n.d., <http://www.ebkids.org/information/what-is-eb.html> (May 24, 2008).

3. Jenny Sundel, "Making a Splash," *Los Angeles Times,* October 7, 2007, *Epidermolysis Bullosa Medical Research Foundation,* n.d., <http://ebkids.org/spotlight/pdf/events/LATimes-CelEBration_on_the_Pier.pdf> (May 24, 2008).

4. "Cards With a Heart—CelEBrity Cards," *Epidermolysis Bullosa Medical Research Foundation,* n.d., <http://www.ebkids.org/shop/cards.php> (May 24, 2008).

5. Marci Weiner, "Hollywood Beat: Life Rolls on the Hollywood Beat," *Movieweb,* August 2, 2007, <http://www.movieweb.com/news/22/21622.php> (May 24, 2008).

6. Eleanor Ringel Gillespie, review of *50 First Dates,* directed by Peter Segal, *Access Atlanta,* February 12, 2004, <http://www.accessatlanta.com/movies/content/shared/movies/reviews/numbers/50firstdates.html> (May 26, 2008).

7. Kevin Thomas, review of *50 First Dates,* directed by Peter Segal, *Los Angeles Times,* February 13, 2004, <http://www.calendarlive.com/movies/reviews/cl-et-thomas13feb13,2,90 0398.story?coll=cl-mreview> (May 26, 2008).

8. Tom Roston, "Adam Sandler Is . . ." *Premiere,* December 2004/January 2005, p. 112.

9. *50 First Dates,* DVD, directed by Peter Segal (Culver City, Calif.: Sony Pictures, 2004).

10. Roston, p. 180.

11. Leah Rozen, review of *The Longest Yard,* directed by Peter Segal, *People,* June 6, 2005, <http://search.ebscohost.com/> (February 18, 2008).

12. Betty Cortina, "Stop the Presses," *Entertainment Weekly,* June 18, 1999, <http://search.ebscohost.com/> (February 18, 2008).

13. Review of *Click,* directed by Frank Coraci, *Rotten Tomatoes,* n.d., <http://www.rottentomatoes.com/m/click/> (May 27, 2008).

14. Nathan Burstein, "Sandler Donates Playstations to Israel," *Jerusalem Post,* August 17, 2006, <http://www.jpost.com/servlet/Satellite?cid=1154525892122&pagename=JPost%2F JPArticle%2FshowFull> (May 8, 2008).

15. "Adam Sandler," *Jewish United Fund/Jewish Federation of Metropolitan Chicago,* <http://www.juf.org/tweens/celebrity.aspx?id=10850> (May 29, 2008).

16. Oliver Jones, "Adam Sandler . . . Answers Your Questions," *People*, July 23, 2007, <http://search.ebscohost.com/> (February 18, 2008).

17. Ibid.

18. Jack Mathews, "Top 'Reign' Man," *New York Daily News,* March 23, 2007, <http://www.nydailynews.com/entertainment/movies/2007/03/23/2007-03-23_top_reign_man.html> (May 31, 2008).

19. Paul Arendt, review *of Reign Over Me,* directed by Mike Binder, *BBC,* April 18, 2007, <http://www.bbc.co.uk/films/2007/04/16/reign_over_me_2007_review.shtml> (May 31, 2008).

20. Review of *Reign Over Me,* directed by Mike Binder, *Rotten Tomatoes,* n.d., <http://www.rottentomatoes.com/m/reign_over_me/?page=1&critic=approved&sortby=date&name_order=asc&view=#mo> (May 31, 2008).

21. Review of *I Now Pronounce You Chuck and Larry,* directed by Dennis Dugan, *Rotten Tomatoes,* n.d., <http://www.rottentomatoes.com/m/i_now_pronounce_you_chuck_and_larry/> (May 31, 2008).

22. "You Don't Mess With the Zohan," *Box Office Mojo,* 2009, <http://www.boxofficemojo.com/movies/?id=youdontmesswiththezohan.htm> (May 15, 2009).

23. Don Cheadle and Annie Duke, *Ante Up for Africa,* n.d., <http://www.anteupforafrica.org> (May 31, 2008).

24. Ibid.

25. Ibid., <http://www.anteupforafrica.org/2007.html> (May 15, 2009).

26. Personal e-mail from Ante Up for Africa cofounder Norman Epstein, May 9, 2008.

27. Associated Press, "Adam Sandler Donates 41 Million to Manchester Charity," *WCAX.com,* October 25, 2007, <http://www.wcax.com/Global/story.asp?S=7262999> (February 12, 2008).

28. Ibid.

29. Personal phone conversation with Tracy Adams, May 8, 2008.

30. *"The Night of Too Many Stars*—Part 8,"(video clip), *Comedy Central,* April 13, 2008, <http://www.comedycentral.com/videos/index.jhtml?videoId=166218> (May 8, 2008).

31 Ibid.

32. Ibid.

33. Ibid.

34. Ibid.

35. Ibid.

36. Personal e-mail from Dana Marnane, National Director of Communications and Marketing, Autism Speaks, June 6, 2008.

37. "Adam Sandler Likes Messing With You," *USA Today,* June 5, 2008, p. 3D.

38. "Bedtime Stories," *Box Office Mojo,* 2009, <http://www.boxofficemojo.com/movies/?id=bedtimestories.htm> (May 15, 2009).

39. Telephone interview with Mike Clemons, March 7, 2008.

40. "A Conversation With Paul Thomas Anderson and Adam Sandler," *Charlie Rose,* October 10, 2002, <http://www.charlierose.com/view/interview/2341> (May 7, 2008).

Further Reading

Books

Epstein, Dwayne. *Adam Sandler*. San Diego: Lucent, 2004.

Horn, Geoffrey. *Adam Sandler*. Milwaukee: Gareth Stevens, 2005.

Uschan, Michael. *Adam Sandler*. Broomall, Pa.: Mason Crest, 2008.

Internet Addresses

The Official Adam Sandler Site
http://www.adamsandler.com/

Adam Sandler—Yahoo! Movies
http://movies.yahoo.com/movie/
contributor/1800018711

Index

125

Acknowledgments

Many thanks to the following people who allowed me to interview or email them and interrupt their days so I could make this the best book possible: Bill Dow, Kyle McDonough, Mike Clemons, Bob Schiavone, Malcolm Jamal-Warner, Kelly Kerrigan, Jill McDonough, Tom Farley, Norman Epstein, Tracy Adams, and Dana Marnane.